FRAGMENTS OF GENIUS

FRAGMENTS OF GENIUS

The Strange Feats of Idiots Savants

MICHAEL J.A. HOWE

ROUTLEDGE

London and New York

First published 1989 by Routledge
11 New Fetter Lane, London EC4P 4EE
Simultaneously published in the USA and Canada
by Routledge
a division of Routledge, Chapman and Hall, Inc.
29 West 35th Street, New York, NY 10001

Phototypeset in 10pt Baskerville by
Mews Photosetting, Beckenham, Kent
Printed and bound in Great Britain by
Biddles Ltd, Guildford and King's Lynn

British Library Cataloguing in Publication Data

Howe, Michael J.A. (Michael John Anthony), 1940–
Fragments of genius: the strange feats
of idiots savants.
1. Man. Mental disorders. Syndromes
I. Title
616.89′072

Library of Congress Cataloging in Publication Data

Howe, Michael J.A, 1940–
Fragments of genius: the strange feats of idiots
savants / Michael Howe.
p.   cm.
Bibliography: p.
Includes index.
1. Savants (Savant syndrome) 2. Savant syndrome. I. Title.
BF426.H78   1980   89-10380
153,9–dc20   CIP

ISBN 0-415-00781-X

CONTENTS

ILLUSTRATIONS

PREFACE

Unusual individuals are always interesting, but their strangeness often
conceals surprising similarities with people who are not at all abnormal.
One's first reaction to witnessing a person who is undoubtedly mentally
handicapped, but nevertheless capable of formidable intellectual feats,
is to be intrigued by the sheer weirdness of someone whose behaviour
contradicts deep-rooted assumptions about mental abilities and human
intelligence. These people can do things which, it seems, ought not
to be possible at all. Later, it becomes apparent that normal and abnormal people might not be not so very different from each other: the
feats of retarded individuals can serve to draw attention to aspects of
normal functioning which are equally hard to reconcile with some of
our beliefs about human abilities.

I am especially grateful to Julia Smith. My interest in the skills of
mentally handicapped people dates from the day when she first drew
my attention to a remarkable boy who could provide the correct day
of the week for any date you told him. The subsequent investigation
of that boy's feats, described towards the end of Chapter 5, was largely
initiated by her, and she undertook all the delicate testing tasks
involved. By the time Julia and I had gnawed at some length on the
problems encountered in trying to discover just how that boy performed
the remarkable feats he kindly shared with us, I was strongly committed to discovering all I could about these fascinating individuals
who display fragments of genius in the face of forbidding intellectual
limitations.

I must also acknowledge the help of a number of other people. Lorna
Selfe kindly gave me an early version of a, then, unpublished chapter
on the artistic talents of a number of mentally retarded adolescents.
Dick Neisser told me about an important recent investigation that he

ix

and Brett Kahr had just completed. Numerous individuals in Britain, North America and Australia have talked to me about cases they have encountered – even anecdotal accounts of idiots savants can sometimes prove highly valuable. Intellectually, I am also grateful to A. Lewis Hill, whose excellent brief survey of savant skills includes a list of references to the earlier literature that the most extensive computerized data bases cannot match.

Chapter One

INTRODUCTION

Leonard's achievements were impressive. His mastery of the piano was outstanding, and a leading American chamber orchestra often asked him to play the piano at rehearsals. A number of prominent musicians had remarked on the excellence of his technique. As he played, capturing every nuance of the music, his bearded face would display the emotion, strength and concentration of a perfectionist who practised up to nine hours each day in order to achieve the level of performance he demanded of himself. When Leonard listened to music played by others his approach was critical and informed.

He was an excellent sight reader and he also played by ear. Music had begun to interest him very early in his life: even before he learned to talk he would hum tunes that he had heard on the radio, and he had the gift of perfect pitch. His knowledge of music and musicians was impressive. He knew a great deal about many composers and the details of their lives, as well as having an expert's understanding of their compositions.

Although music was his first love, Leonard had other talents. A tall, healthy man, whose well-to-do parents had both attended university, he had an outstanding capacity to remember written information. On one occasion he was asked to read a couple of three-page articles about George Washington and Thomas Edison. After one silent reading of the article on Washington he recited it aloud, word for word and without a single error. He gave a word-perfect recitation of the Edison passage after reading it twice. He also had a large fund of biographical knowledge about many prominent individuals outside the world of music, and he had a knack of remembering the exact time and place of events in the life of his family. Whenever one of his relatives was uncertain about the details of something that had happened in the past, Leonard's memory could be relied upon.

Lionel, in sharp contrast with Leonard, was a total failure. Lionel was a mentally retarded forty-year-old whose behaviour was inadequate and oddly childlike. Sometimes he would dart around with objects balanced on his head, or gesticulate strangely, or kiss anything that he happened to notice, or make funny faces, or speak into mirrors, or suddenly begin an odd dance movement. At times he could be boorish, licking his plate after a meal, pushing strangers out of his way, or belching and farting in public. He was lazy in his personal habits: it took him half an hour to dress himself and he never had a shower unless he was told to do so. Whenever he dressed himself his mother had to lay out the garments in advance, otherwise Lionel put on the first items of clothing that met his eye. He showed no interest at all in sexual matters and never seemed at all aware of the distinction between male and female. He had only the shallowest relationships with other people, although he appeared to be fond of his mother, and he enjoyed the company of his dog. Even so, if one of the family was absent for a day or so he would forget all about that person and give no sign of missing them.

Lionel's behaviour could be excessively rigid, the slightest disturbance to his normal routine causing him great distress. If a meal was not served at precisely the usual time he would become highly agitated and refuse to eat. On one occasion when his teacher arrived at the house fifteen minutes earlier than usual, Lionel was so upset that he refused to open the door and let him in.

The precise cause of Lionel's retardation remained a mystery, but a number of neurologists, psychiatrists and psychologists who his parents consulted at one time or another agreed that he had contracted epidemic encephalitis (disease of the brain) soon after birth, causing permanent damage. That he was mentally handicapped was apparent by the time Lionel reached his first birthday. He did not begin to talk until he was five years old. Even when he became an adult his speech remained abnormally high-pitched and childish, having a kind of sing-song quality.

At the age of forty, Lionel's mental performance was roughly on a par with a normal ten-year-old's. He eventually learned to read but never seemed to have a real understanding of the content. If a passage of writing was preceded by a summary, he failed to comprehend why the author had repeated himself. Lionel could not do any task that required him to think abstractly: when his intelligence was tested he failed at those items which involved detecting similarities or differences, or completing unfinished sentences, or showing an understanding of the meaning of proverbs, or telling a story in his own words. Tasks that demanded good reasoning ability totally defeated him, as did intelligence test items designed to assess such skills as copying from memory, arranging objects in their correct positions, finding reasons for everyday events, or demonstrating any of the symbolic or coding abilities that normal people use in everyday life. In short, Lionel was mentally handicapped to the extent that he had to rely on other people to provide care and protection for daily living.

As you may have guessed, the men I have called Leonard and Lionel were actually one and the same person. Surprising as it may seem, Leonard, the masterly and admired musician, was precisely the same individual as the mentally retarded Lionel, the childish and incompetent person who could tolerate no changes or surprises. The man who had no real understanding of the meaning of written materials was the very same individual as the one whose knowledge of music and musicians was so enviably striking. The accounts of Leonard and Lionel have been taken from a single case history, reported by Anne Anastasi and Raymond Levee (1960). I have simply recounted the positive achievements of the one individual, ascribing them to Leonard, and I have attributed the same man's deficiencies to Lionel: only the name has been altered. In Leonard/Lionel, retardation in most aspects of mental life, and outstanding talent in certain restricted spheres, coexisted within a single person.

We are not used to encountering such a contrast in levels of ability within a single individual. The discrepancy is alarming: it presents something of a paradox. How can someone be at once so outstandingly talented and deeply retarded? Such a huge variation in the quality of mental life between the different areas of intellectual activity within one individual is alien to everyday experience. People like Leonard/Lionel are not simply rare: there is also an upside-down quality about them. It is not unusual to encounter someone who plays tennis well but is a poor reader, or who cooks superbly and knits appallingly, but the evidence of most people's experiences encourages us to believe that everyone operates with a degree of consistency, at least where mental abilities are concerned. We tend to think of individuals as being more or less able in general; and we take it for granted that knowing something about someone's broad level of intelligence makes it possible to predict with fair accuracy how well that person will deal with any of a variety of different tasks.

Such assumptions normally serve us quite well but they are rudely shattered when we encounter the mysterious contradictions of someone like Leonard/Lionel, or others who are like him in being mentally retarded but possessing striking mental skills. They are usually known as 'idiots savants' in medical and psychological journals. They present clear proof that pronounced mental retardation and impressive mental abilities can coexist in one person at the same time. And, as we shall see, the evidence of their fragmented achievements also contradicts certain of our most basic assumptions about the nature of human intelligence.

Most people, psychologists included, are baffled by these remarkable people. Their feats are hard to believe. Our everyday experience tells us that everyone possesses a fixed amount of intelligence and that, by and large, a person's intelligence level places firm constraints on mental achievements. The discovery that people exist for whom these assumptions are definitely not true forces us to reconsider some of our views about the nature of human abilities. It contradicts the widely accepted belief that intelligence functions as a unitary capacity that underlies a range of different abilities, placing firm limits on what a person can actually do.

As it happens, the only evidence for such a belief is in the form of correlations between different skills. Because, in most people, the observed level of performance at one mental ability helps us to predict the level of performance at other mental abilities, we conclude that different abilities must go hand in hand, controlled by some all-embracing capacity, which we usually choose to call intelligence. Reports of idiots savants demonstrate that such a conclusion is not inevitable: if it was, people in whom different mental abilities are independent of one another would never be found.

That the patterns of achievements and deficits displayed by certain mentally retarded individuals may have broad implications for our understanding of the way in which human abilities are arranged and controlled is a matter that will be examined in later chapters. The fact that savants' feats provide one form of evidence contradicting every-day assumptions about the centrality of measured intelligence provides a reason for believing that it may be valuable to take a fresh look at other kinds of information concerning the organization of abilities in human beings. As we shall see, the evidence of achievements by individuals who are not mentally retarded supplements that of idiots savants' feats. These other kinds of evidence give further proof that many separate mental abilities can exist in relative isolation, to a large extent independently of a person's measured intelligence.

In some respects the case of Leonard/Lionel is not at all unique. People in whom highly developed talents exist against a general background of mental retardation are certainly very unusual, but hundreds of such cases have been reported. There are a few retarded people who, like Leonard/Lionel, are extremely good at music. Some mentally handicapped individuals can recall pages of information, word perfect, from a timetable or a telephone directory. Other idiots savants are highly skilled at mental arithmetic, and some perform difficult calculations at amazing speed. A few mentally retarded children have artistic abilities that are remarkably superior to the skills encountered in any normal children of the same age. Some retarded people are immensely skilled at model-building. Substantial numbers of idiots savants perform remarkable feats with calendar dates: if they are told someone's day of birth, or a date in the future, such people will rapidly calculate the correct day of the week.

DESCRIPTIVE TERMS

'Idiot savant' is the term that has most frequently been used to designate mentally handicapped individuals who are capable of outstanding achievements at particular tasks, but scientists reporting on these people have also introduced a number of alternative labels. These include 'talented imbecile', 'parament', 'talented ament', 'retarded savant', 'schizophrenic savant', and 'autistic savant'. Some authors have used lengthier descriptive terms, such as 'children with circumscribed interest patterns'. Others write of 'the savant syndrome'.

None of these words and phrases is entirely satisfactory as a descriptive term. 'Savant' is not ideal, although it is hard to think of a better label that is equally succinct. Only in a severely restricted range of circumstances can these individuals be regarded as at all 'wise', and they are often totally inadequate at the practical skills required for daily living. Perhaps, however, 'savant' is less objectionable if (following Hill 1978) one translates it from the French not as 'wise' but as 'person of knowledge'.

The word 'idiot' is particularly unsatisfactory, and not only because it is now used as a form of abuse. Even when that word had a legitimate technical meaning as a (now obsolete) classifying label, it designated a much narrower spectrum of feeble-mindedness than is actually occupied by those mentally retarded people who display special skills. (In Britain, an idiot was said to be a person whose IQ was less than 20, indicating a level of mental functioning inferior to that of a normal two-year-old, and considerably beneath that of the majority of the people to whom the term idiots savant has in fact been applied. According to the Mental Deficiency Act of 1913, idiots were persons in whom there existed mental defectiveness of such a degree that they could not guard themselves against common physical dangers.)

Of all the above terms '(mentally) retarded savant' is perhaps the least unsatisfactory. But since those who have written about the people I describe in this book have most often chosen to call them 'idiots savants', some confusion might be caused by abandoning the familiar terminology altogether. I shall write of both 'idiots savants' and 'retarded savants', interchangeably. Whatever the chosen forms of words, it is important to be clear that whilst having some kind of descriptive terminology is undoubtedly useful for broadly classifying people, any suggestion that the chosen term can also serve to explain their attributes should be resisted. It would be unwise, for instance, to make any explanatory inferences when terms such as 'autistic savant' or 'schizophrenic savant' are encountered. They are useful descriptive labels but really no more than that.

When we start to explain how and why some of the most striking feats are accomplished, it will be necessary to tread rather carefully through a minefield of logical and empirical obstacles to genuine understanding. A point to be emphasized at the outset is that there definitely does not exist any one simple explanation of all the puzzles that retarded savants pose. That is not to deny that it may be worth looking for common explanatory themes that link the different accomplishments that such people display.

SAVANT SKILLS

Many case histories testify to the remarkable achievements of the mentally handicapped people who have been described as idiots savants. These people are very uncommon, but any reader who has worked in schools or institutions that cater for the mentally handicapped will probably have encountered at least one or two individuals with very special talents. Furthermore, retarded savants can be found in every continent: Xiaowen Han, a psychologist from Beijing, described to me a fourteen-year-old mentally retarded boy who performs impressive memorization feats and can give the correct page number for any Chinese character in a 400-page student's dictionary. As we have seen, the accomplishments of retarded savants take a variety of forms, and whilst some savants have just one special skill it is more usual for a single individual to excel at several activities, all standing out in sharp contrast to the limited and often tragically restricted behaviour of a mentally retarded person.

Some retarded people have shared Leonard/Lionel's talent for music. The recorded case histories include instances of pronounced musical accomplishments in individuals whose mental handicap was much more severe than his. For instance, there is a published report of a twenty-three-year-old Minnesota woman living in an institution for the feeble-minded (Owens and Grimm 1941) whose intellectual limitations were so extreme that she made little progress at learning to speak (her few words being repetitive and indistinct). Her mental age was assessed at only two years and nine months. Yet without having received any musical instruction at all she could play on the piano any piece of music that people would sing or hum to her. She regularly played hymn tunes for the other inmates of her institution, and she entertained them with popular music heard on the radio, which she always reproduced in the correct key.

Other retarded savants have been exceptional in the visual arts, displaying impressive abilities at painting and drawing. Particularly remarkable is the case of a mentally retarded young child named Nadia, whose amazingly competent animal drawings are reproduced in a book by Lorna Selfe (1977). From the age of three years Nadia produced drawings of animals which depicted reality with an uncanny accuracy that is quite unknown in the artistic attempts of normal children. Lorna Selfe's investigation established that in this exceptional case the very absence of normal mental abilities may have contributed to Nadia's being able to display representative skills that are precluded by the thinking processes of more intelligent young children.

Impressive feats of remembering are relatively common in retarded savants. The particular kinds of information that different individuals can recall vary considerably: some retarded savants have specialized in telephone directories, others in railway timetables, sporting results, the names of people or places, or (as in Leonard/Lionel's case) biographical information. At the beginning of the present century there lived a man who would meet all the trains that passed through Oxford, his home town in the American state of Mississippi (Byrd 1920). He memorized all the engine numbers, which he wrote down in a notebook, together with other kinds of information, such as station names. These also he was able to recall.

Another mentally retarded man knew the population figures for every town in the USA. He would recite the names of about 2,000 American hotels, together with their locations and the number of rooms they had available (Jones 1926). He could also state the distances between New York and all other American cities, the distance between each town and the main city in the same state, and the names of all the county seats throughout the USA. Further facts that this man could recite included statistical information concerning 3,000 mountains and rivers, and details of well over 2,000 discoveries and inventions. When asked about population statistics, not only could he state the number of people living in a particular town, but if he was given a population figure (from the 1920 US Census) he would say the name of the town or city having that number of citizens. For example, to the question, '78,684?', he answered, correctly, 'San Diego'. In the case of yet another idiot savant, when she was a young girl her father read to her the first three pages of the Boston telephone directory. Afterwards, she remembered all the numbers and for several years she remained able to recall them.

In each of the above instances, although the person's knowledge was impressive there existed rigid limits on what the individual could actually *do* with the information that was remembered. Typically, retarded savants can recall material only if it is cued in a particular way. For instance, one mentally handicapped London man knew every single line of every hymn in the book that was used in the church he attended, but he could only recite a particular hymn if he was first given the appropriate number in the hymn book. The kinds of fragmentary cues that might serve a normal person as effective aids for recall – the title for instance, or part of the first line – were no help to this man at all. Another restriction is that the retarded person is rarely able to combine separate items in memory, or to discern qualities they may have in common. Thus one nine-year-old boy could correctly answer both 'Into what does the Mississippi River flow?' and 'Into what does the Rio Grande River flow?' by saying 'The Gulf of Mexico' in each case, but he was struck dumb by the question, 'What two rivers do you know that flow into the Gulf of Mexico?' (Parker 1917).

8

Another skill that certain retarded savants possess is the ability to perform difficult calculations by mental arithmetic. Some mentally retarded people (and a few individuals having normal or superior intelligence) have been successful as 'lightning' mental calculators, having the ability to solve arithmetic tasks at immense speed. By way of illustration, one blind young man who lived in a French mental asylum could supply the cube root of any six-digit number in six seconds, or the square root of any four-digit number in four seconds. When he was asked to calculate the number of grains of corn in each of sixty-four boxes, assuming that one piece of grain was placed in the first of the boxes, two in the second, four in the third, eight in the fourth, and so on, he correctly answered that the eighteenth box would contain 131,072 grains of corn, the twenty-fourth 8,368,608 and the forty-eighth 140,737,355,328. It took him just 45 seconds to calculate the total number of grains of corn in all sixty-four boxes.

One of the most intriguing of all the mental skills displayed by retarded savants, and perhaps the best known, is calendar calculating. Typically, if a person who can do calendar calculations is told the date of someone's birthday he will immediately state the day of the week on which the date fell. He will do the same for any past or future date, within limits. Some idiots savants can perform calendar data calculations of this kind for any day within a span of hundreds of years. Often they can answer questions that demand further calendar calculating abilities. For instance, when I asked one thirteen-year-old retarded boy to tell me the years on which 14 September falls on a Wednesday, with hardly any delay he rattled off a long sequence of dates, all correct, some of them from past years and others falling in the future.

How do they do it? Calendar calculating almost certainly depends upon a person being able to recall large bodies of information about dates. Also, some elementary arithmetic skills seem to be essential. Yet it has not been at all easy to discover exactly how retarded savants actually manage their calendar calculations. Furthermore, there is also the question of why they do this particular skill: there is no obvious explanation of the fact that a high proportion (around a third) of those retarded savants whose achievements have been recorded happen to include calendar calculating among their exceptional feats.

There are procedures that people of normal intelligence can follow in order to perform some of the skills demonstrated by calendar calculators. Written descriptions of such methods can be located without too much difficulty in certain handbooks, diaries, encyclopedias and other published sources. But it is hard to imagine how access to published instructions could be possible for the majority of the feeble-minded people, usually institutionalized and illiterate, who perform this feat. Remarkably enough, it seems likely that almost all idiot savant calendar calculators have succeeded in developing their own individual methods, in some instances with the aid of conventional calendars or perpetual calendar devices.

Like other retarded savants, calendar calculators often have additional talents. Not surprisingly, they can usually recall large numbers of dates, and some of these people can remember events that happened on every single day over a period of years. Occasionally, for instance, a person can recall long sequences of daily weather reports. The thirteen-year-old boy whose calendar calculating I have already mentioned could also remember the birthday of every single pupil and member of staff at the school he attended. Of course, knowledge of a large number of particular dates is extremely helpful, if not essential, for performing calculations involving calendar dates.

Over the years, many other remarkable idiot savant performances have been encountered. These include certain practical skills, such as the carefully planned and executed feats of model building achieved by a man named James Henry Pullen, who died in 1916 at the age of seventy-eight and was known as 'the Genius of Earlswood Asylum' (the institution where he lived). His masterpiece was a ten-foot model of the nineteenth-century steamship, *The Great Eastern*. He constructed it with the most careful attention to every minute detail: Pullen himself designed and made all the numerous parts, including over a million wooden pins and thousands of copper rivets. Nowadays, impressive feats of model-building by mentally handicapped individuals are still rare, but I learned only recently of a retarded boy who builds elaborate dolls' houses, made from cardboard, which demonstrate an astounding talent for planning and design.

Other achievements by retarded savants include some oddly impressive feats of imitation. In a few instances these have involved the accurate reproduction of a lengthy spoken passage in a foreign language that the individual could not understand. Certain of the skills demonstrated by retarded people are remarkable mainly for their bizarreness. One of the weirdest reported cases was that of a man who, although profoundly retarded to the extent that he could not even dress himself or speak a single word, had the curious ability to spin corrugated metal dustpans and other objects on the index fingers of either of his hands (Rife and Snyder 1931).

It would take a long time to describe all the different achievements that retarded savants have demonstrated, let alone explain them. No explanation is likely to be satisfactory unless it casts light on how a feat or skill was first acquired. In order to make progress towards understanding how such people gain their unusual skills it will be necessary to discover more about the individuals concerned than can be learned from simply listing their feats. It would certainly be useful to obtain some knowledge of the characters and personalities of the individual people whose achievements interest us. What are they like? What kinds of people are they? Do they share any characteristics of personality or temperament, other than mental handicap? Can their curious patterns of abilities and disabilities be related to other aspects of retardation? Are there ways in which a retarded person's disabilities can make it easier rather than more difficult to gain certain skills?

When we are endeavouring to discover how individual retarded savants have been able to acquire their skills, it would be especially valuable to know how and why they were motivated to undertake the necessary learning, which may have required the person to sustain careful concentration over very lengthy periods of time. In order to gather some of the background information which makes it possible to begin to answer questions that are central to an understanding of the talents encountered in retarded savants, we shall examine, in Chapter 2, the actual lives of some of the mentally retarded individuals whose striking achievements have come to the attention of psychological researchers.

MENTAL RETARDATION AND SAVANT SKILLS

Accounts of the highly impressive skills of retarded savants have sometimes been met with a degree of scepticism on the part of psychologists and other professionals, partly because widely held ideas about the nature of mental retardation and common beliefs about the organization of intelligence leave no room for the possibility that a person who is deeply retarded in most respects can at the same time possess remarkable talents. Even though the sheer quantity of reliable evidence is far too great for total disbelief in the phenomena to have been maintained, traces of that scepticism are still to be discerned in two frequent reactions to accounts that describe the activities of retarded savants.

11

One kind of sceptical response is to say that striking as their feats undoubtedly are, so-called retarded savants are in fact not really mentally retarded in a fundamental sense, but are more accurately seen as being people who are handicapped in ways that prevent normal social activities and communication with others. The suggestion is that such individuals are actually intelligent people, despite all appearances to the contrary.

This view raises a number of interesting issues. Obtaining a realistic indication of the degree to which an individual is mentally handicapped is not nearly so simple as it might appear. In most case histories, the sole objective index of mental functioning is in the form of an IQ test score. These tests are quite effective for assessing the kinds of skills that make for success at a conventional school, but they are not particularly sensitive to differences in the kinds of abilities that are important in the day-to-day lives of mentally retarded individuals. The difficulties of assessment are compounded by the fact that whereas the quality of the environment provided by the institutions which the individuals, described in the published reports of idiots savants, have attended may be very satisfactory in many respects, such institutional environments are notoriously ineffective for producing high levels of performance at intelligence tests. Bronfenbrenner (1979) illustrates this point in an anecdote about the institution for 'the feeble-minded' where his father worked as a neuropathologist. Occasionally children who were perfectly normal would be accidently committed to the institution, and it would take several weeks to unwind the red tape necessary for their release. By then, however,

> After a few weeks as one of eighty inmates in a cottage with two matrons, their scores on the intelligence tests administered as a compulsory part of the discharge process proved them mentally deficient. (Bronfenbrenner 1979: xii)

My raising the question of whether or not certain individuals are genuinely retarded may be taken to imply that this word has a precision that it does not actually possess. In fact, the many individuals who may legitimately be designated as mentally retarded form an enormously diverse population: many of them have very little in common with one another. It would be quite wrong to regard mentally retarded people as forming a coherent group, about whom generalizations can confidentaly be made. John Belmont cautions his readers that retardation

12

is a complicated social judgement embodied in a single word. It is a label applied to people who have any of a huge range of physical, intellectual or social qualities that fail to conform to societal expectation, and the only thing that even approaches universally distinguishing people who are called retarded is that they behave like people much younger than they. But be careful. Do not assume that any particular retarded person necessarily appears to be younger in all ways, nor that all appear to be younger in any one way. (Belmont 1978: 155)

As a rule, it would be wise to assume that the intelligence test scores reported in published descriptions of retarded savants provide only the crudest of guides to the actual level of individuals' mental functioning.

Concerning the suggestion that handicaps suffered by retarded savants may be primarily social rather than intellectual, it is true to say that some (but not all) savants have personalities which might be described as being to varying extents 'schizophrenic', 'autistic', or 'psychotic'. Moreover, there are undoubtedly some genuine differences between the retarded people to whom these adjectives do and do not apply. However, particularly in the case of austistic individuals, who form a proportion of the people who exhibit savant skills, there are strong grounds for arguing that retardation is no less real than it is in other people who are mentally handicapped.

The second kind of sceptical response is to suggest that the achievements of idiots savants are not, after all, so very astounding, and that any of the skills can be readily performed by any normal individual who is so inclined. Concerning this view, it can be said that some of the achievements of retarded savants can indeed be duplicated by people of normal intelligence who are prepared to commit enough time and patience to a task which they are likely to find exceedingly boring. But some of the feats definitely cannot be matched by any normal individual. There are various reasons for this, some purely intellectual and others involving motivational considerations. The retarded child artist, Nadia (see Chapter 6), is one example of an individual in whom the very absence of normal cognitive processes may have had the effect of removing barriers that make it impossible for intelligent children to produce the realistic pictorial reproductions at which she excels. That is not to say that the cognitive abilities she lacks are superfluous: they are certainly essential for a real understanding of the meaning of objects in the world and the relationships between them. Normal children understand the meanings of things, but Nadia does not.

Certain feats by retarded savants that involve literal memorization of vast bodies of information provide further demonstrations of the fact that the absence of normal information processing abilities may sometimes permit a mentally handicapped individual to undertake tasks that would not be possible for an intelligent person. In such instances the mental processing which takes place when a retarded person perceives things is restricted in comparison with the more extensive and deeper cognitive processing that normally occurs when people perceive items or events. An outcome of normal perceptual processing is that a person forms meaningful and abstract representations of the information that is perceived. These are retained in memory. One consequence of the more superficial mental processing that may occur in a retarded person is that only the surface attributes of items are processed. This can lead to superior recall of information about the physical forms of things. For example, the sounds of a foreign language may be better recalled by someone whose attention is focused on the sound and not the meaning. But the absence of deep processing has a heavy psychological price, involving a failure to retain the meanings of events and their implications. The limitations of the concrete memorizing achievements of some idiots savants are not totally unlike the restrictions that exist when sounds are retained on magnetic tape. Compared with normal human memory, there is the advantage of greater surface accuracy, but this occurs at the expense of all the abilities that depend upon meaningful understanding; for example, being able to find and use particular items of information.

Motivational factors provide further barriers that inhibit intelligent people from matching some of the achievements of retarded individuals. Boredom is one. Normal people find it impossible to concentrate for lengthy periods of time on the surface qualities of what is perceived, in the face of the competition for attention from the more meaningful, and therefore more interesting, events that are encountered in everyday life. It is possible, by imposing conditions of sensory deprivation, to eliminate some of the forms of stimulation that normally make it difficult for a person to sustain attention to the kinds of narrow and repetitive activities that retarded savants seem to enjoy, such as memorizing timetables or calendar calculating. Similar conditions may also be produced by lengthy incarceration in isolated prison environments. But even under the most extreme circumstances of sensory deprivation, any normal person who is reasonably imaginative will differ greatly from retarded individuals in the extent and complexity of the internal stimulation that is produced by thoughts and memories. Most normal people find solace in their own thoughts if they are trapped in an environment that is devoid of interest. A mentally retarded individual, lacking such inner resources, may nevertheless require some mental stimulation: but for that person the need may be satisfied by forms of information that more intelligent individuals would find meaningless and devoid of interest.

It was the strange combination of extraordinary powers and sad limitations encountered in retarded savants which first brought these curious and bizarrely fragmented people to the author's attention. My interest in them was initially sustained by the wish to understand their baffling contradictions. How do such people manage to do the various things they achieve? How are their feats possible, in the absence of thinking and learning capacities that are virtually taken for granted as being necessary for all but the simplest mental tasks? An aim of cognitive psychology is to cast light on the systems of mental processing operations that underlie various kinds of behaviour in humans. In the search for greater clarity, retarded savants' unusual arrays of skills and disabilities, and their capacity to succeed at certain feats without possessing certain cognitive abilities that might otherwise appear to form an essential mental background for those feats, can contribute useful clues. In such people, the very absence of the mental abilities that are encountered in most of the normal people who possess a skill that is being investigated provides information that helps us to discriminate between those mental capacities that are essential for the skill and those which, although usually present in someone possessing that skill, are not in fact essential for it.

But in attempting to discover how retarded savants are able to achieve mental feats without having the intellectual capacities possessed by those non-retarded people who are capable of similar feats, we are inevitably led into the broader and more fundamental questions that I raised earlier, concerning the operation of intelligence and the organization and control of human abilities. If, in retarded savants, particular mental talents can flourish in the absence of normal levels of measured intelligence, does this mean that the governing role of human intelligence over normal people's abilities is only a weak one, or even non-existent? Is it possible that the widely accepted point of view in which broad intellectual ability, or intelligence, is seen as having a controlling function over specific mental abilities is a false and misleading one, and utterly wrong? Have we been misled by the correlations that are generally found between individuals' different abilities? These have encouraged psychologists to believe that the different aspects of human cognition always operate with a degree of co-ordination, under some kind of central control. Is it possible that the real explanation of the observed correlations between normal individuals' different skills is simply that the different skills have common elements, or rest on identical sub-skills?

Studies investigating idiots savants can provide information that is vital if questions like these are to be answered. Further sources of valuable data on these issues include records of individuals who are not mentally retarded but are remarkable or extraordinary in other ways. For instance, descriptions of individuals having normal or above-average intelligence who possess rare skills, or unusual patterns of abilities and deficits, are especially helpful. So, too, are descriptions of people whose abilities have been selectively impaired, following brain damage or disease. Information about mental prodigies who have reached high levels of excellence in particular spheres at an unusually young age can be especially valuable. All these very different kinds of individuals contribute additional evidence concerning the extent to which it is possible for abilities that are usually found to accompany one another when they are measured in normal people to have an independent, autonomous existence in human cognition. In later chapters, a considerable amount of data from extraordinary individuals who are not mentally retarded will be introduced, adding detail and clarity to the new picture of the structure and organization of abilities in humans that first begins to emerge from the investigations of the striking feats of retarded savants.

In short, although much of this book will be concerned with trying to discover how retarded savants are able to do the unusual feats they perform, we shall inevitably be drawn into examining broader issues and implications. The book makes use of the insights to be gained from examining the activities of these oddly remarkable individuals in order to shed a fresh light upon the nature of human competence and reshape our understanding of the structure and organization of ordinary people's mental abilities. The findings which initially seem to be so impressive simply because they point to the existence of people whose juxtapositions of talents and limitations are fascinating and bizarre turn out to have vital wider implications as well, redirecting our thinking about the operation of mental skills.

The form of this book broadly reflects these concerns. Chapter 2 puts some flesh on the present chapter's brief descriptions of retarded savants. It looks at a few of them in depth, as individual human beings, and discusses the suggestion that savant skills are especially likely to be found in autistic individuals. Remembering is an essential component of most of the feats of retarded savants, and the aim of Chapter 3 is to describe and explain some of the memory skills. Chapter 4 continues the attempt to explain savant skills. It also draws attention to the fact that discoveries about the feats of mentally retarded savants have important implications for our knowledge of ordinary people's abilities: a main theme of the book is that the achievements of savants contradict widely accepted beliefs that are central to our understanding of the organization of human abilities. The achievements force us to re-examine some of our basic thinking about the nature of human ability. Chapter 5 looks at the remarkable calendar feats that are performed by some mentally retarded people. It reports on the efforts of various investigators, including the author, to describe the cognitive skills that underlie the ability to solve problems about past and future calendar dates and discover how the individuals concerned have been able to achieve their feats. Chapter 6 describes some remarkable achievements in the visual arts by mentally retarded individuals. These include feats by mentally retarded children which are incomparably superior to the achievements of the most intelligent normal children. Chapter 7, which concludes the book, raises some questions about extraordinary abilities in individuals of all kinds. The chapter draws attention to some intriguing similarities to be seen in individuals who, in most respects, are very different from each other, and it gives further proof that discoveries about savants and progress in explaining their feats have implications for people of all levels of ability.

I have *not* tried to provide an exhaustive survey of all the research that has examined savants' abilities. Some of their skills receive more attention than others. For example, whilst calendar calculating is investigated rather thoroughly, certain abilities – such as musical ones – are not at all closely examined. (A useful bibliography listing recent investigations of musical abilities in mentally retarded savants is provided by Darold Treffert, 1989.)

Much of the following chapter is taken up by just two fairly detailed accounts of individual retarded savants. The main reason for including these descriptions is to convey to the reader some idea of what these people are actually like. The descriptions give a reasonably full indication of some of the personality characteristics and temperaments of those mentally retarded people who perform feats such as the ones that have been mentioned in this chapter. The accounts also contain information about the lives the individuals have led, and show how their skills may begin to emerge and are subsequently expanded and modified, typically over time-spans of several years.

Like everyone else, each mentally retarded person is unique, but in comparing different retarded savants it is usually possible to see some points of similarity. Each of the individuals to be described in Chapter 2 is in some respects one of a kind but in other respects fairly typical of those retarded people who are capable of similar feats.

Chapter Two

SOME REMARKABLE INDIVIDUALS

The major part of this chapter is devoted to fairly detailed descriptions of particular retarded savants. Only two individuals are described at length. By giving relatively full accounts of these people, and including biographical information about their lives, personalities and temperaments, as well as their intellectual achievements and deficiencies, I aim to communicate some idea of what kinds of real human beings are behind the unusual feats reported in the published case-histories of retarded savants.

RICHARD

By the time Richard's fourth birthday arrived his mother had noticed that he would say 'you' when he should have said 'I', and 'yes' instead of 'no'. In some respects he was decidedly backward. He could not manage to hold his knife and fork correctly, nor was he able to catch a ball or even turn the knob of his bedroom door. Going to the bathroom on his own was impossible. Unlike most small boys Richard never plagued his mother with questions beginning with 'Why?', and he did not imitate other people or play with the toys he had been given.

Richard's infancy had seemed normal enough. He came from a professional family in which mental defects were unknown. His mother, who had been a school teacher, was to devote much of her time to teaching Richard, throughout his childhood. Apart from the occasional cough and cold he was very healthy. He ate and slept normally and his early toilet training proceeded satisfactorily. At six months he appeared to be a normal baby: he could sit up and was beginning to make the sounds that usually lead to early speech. In the following month his first tooth appeared. At ten months he could stand, and he walked at fifteen months. The only thing that seemed at all abnormal about Richard in his first year was that he kicked his feet rather frequently and moved his hands and fingers unusually often.

By eighteen months, however, there were worrying signs in his behaviour. He talked no more than he had done six months earlier, and his very small vocabulary was not increasing at the normal rate. He often seemed to be restless and he easily became frightened, and had difficulty in getting to sleep.

Soon after his parents had begun to suspect that Richard might be mentally retarded they noticed some remarkable features in his behaviour. In Richard's third year he started to become extremely interested in music: he quickly recognized melodies he had heard, and he learned the titles of numerous records. Also, he appeared to enjoy counting things. He would count the keys on the piano, or items in the wallpaper, or any suitable objects in the room he was occupying. He invented odd word games, which he played with great enjoyment. For instance, on seeing one object he might rapidly say the name of an associated item, or another word which sounded similar.

By now Richard had become a very difficult child. He developed sudden tantrums, sometimes when he could not find something he wanted, but often for no apparent reason at all. The trantrums would cease as suddenly as they had appeared. He continued to become frightened often and readily. Any sudden movement or sound could startle him, and after he had once been scared by a particular event such as the sound of thunder or the chiming of a clock he would quickly acquire a conditioned response of fear or terror. Afterwards, he would start to scream, especially if it was night-time, at any repetition of the sight or sound that had frightened him. So intense were his fears of animals that until he was twelve years of age he could never be persuaded to step outside the house on his own.

Richard's social skills were meagre. For a short time his mother tried sending him to a nursery, but he never played with the other children and he gave the impression of being quite unaware of their presence. He ignored children and adults alike. His mother, from who he refused to be separated, was the sole person to whom he would listen or with whom he would try to communicate. As he grew older he gained some new skills but his progress was very uneven. He learned the letters of the alphabet, and could recognize them even if they were upside-down. By his fifth birthday Richard could spell at least one hundred short words. He was clearly fascinated by numbers: as well as being able to add he could count by twos or by fours, and even by sixteens. Yet he could not concentrate at all on tasks which did not fascinate him. He was incapable of studying or trying to memorize school tasks: he ignored his teachers' efforts to make him concentrate. He seemed quite unable to learn from instruction, despite his demonstrated ability to assimilate those verbal and numerical items that happened to catch his attention. Even so, he continued to develop his musical abilities, and music acquired for him the power to elicit some of the emotional responses, including weeping, that were so conspicuously absent in his everyday social encounters.

At the age of seven years Richard began to develop some calendar skills. By this time the oddity of many of his activities was becoming increasingly noticeable. Richard spoke to other people very infrequently, often reacting to questions by simply repeating them. He would usually ignore people around him and remain absorbed in his own activity, which might be dancing, or pounding on the wall, or waving his hands about, or even rolling on the floor. At these times he seemed to all intents oblivious to everything except what he was doing.

Yet whenever someone mentioned to him a day of the week, or a date, or a month he immediately appeared to become a far more rational child. He gained an intense interest in a calendar he was given, and soon after learning the names of the months and the numbers of days in each of them he managed to memorize sufficient information to be able to supply the correct day of the week for every single date in the current year, and the following year as well.

As time advanced Richard made further progress. He became calmer, less unpredictable, and better at controlling his fears. He gradually began to take more interest in other children, and on some occasions he even played with them. His musical skills continued to increase. When Richard was aged eleven, he was subjected to a detailed psychological investigation, which continued over a period of several years, culminating in a lengthy and penetrating report by Martin Scheerer, Eva Rothmann and Kurt Goldstein (1945), on which the present account is based. The investigators were able to persuade Richard to co-operate with them by attempting a number of mental tests, including ones that assessed intelligence.

Scheerer and his colleagues found that Richard's global Intelligence Quotient (when he was tested at the age of eleven and again at fifteen) was around 50, placing his scores in the lowest one per cent of those gained by children of similar age. However, on a few of the sub-tests he performed at or near the level of an average child of his age. For instance, he did fairly well at tasks which required him to count or to retain numerical information, to retain sentences or digits in memory for short periods, to identify pictures or to make simple associations between word items. But Richard failed badly at all those sub-tests that required him to comprehend or reason, or to detect spatial relationships. Hence he could not remember stories and he was unable to answer questions asking why certain events took place. He could not recognize similarities or differences between items, or notice absurdities in word or picture materials. For example, when questioned on a picture absurdity test depicting a man holding an umbrella upside down on a rainy day, Richard simply could not see what was wrong. Nor could he give a proper answer to a question asking how wood and coal are alike. He replied with the curious statement that cables are made out of wood and coal comes out of the cellar.

Richard's responses to the questions that tested his ability to detect similarities between items seemed to demonstrate a primitive kind of thought that reflected a capacity to detect associations between items but which was highly egocentric and concrete. All his thoughts were closely related to his own personal experiences and tied to particular happenings. For example, when he was asked to state the similarity between a ship and an automobile, Richard said, 'I sail with a ship and an automobile can run over', and when he was required to describe the difference between a stone and an egg, he replied 'I eat an egg and I throw a stone' (Scheerer, Rothmann and Goldstein, 1945: 10). His replies gave no indication of the reflective and abstract kinds of reasoning that are assessed by tests of word similarities and differences. Richard could not sort objects into colours, and he was also unable to obey the request to point to the longest of a group of items. He quite failed to understand the concepts 'short' and 'long', although he did have some comprehension of 'big' and 'small'.

In addition to being unable to group objects on the basis of their meaningful qualities, Richard could not generalize at all. Similarly, his understanding was totally literal: he could not grasp the metaphorical or abstract meaning of anything. On one occasion a member of the team of researchers investigating Richard said to him, 'Goodbye, my son'. Richard immediately responded, 'I'm not your son'. And when he was given a test of verbal analogies, to the item, 'The point of a cane is blunt, the knife is —— ', he replied, 'hurts'.

He had no answer at all for some fairly simple items in the analogy test (for example, 'Water is to drink as air is to —— ', 'Potato is to vegetable as veal is to —— '). He answered other easy questions incorrectly. For example, to 'Hat is to head as shoe is to —— ' he answered 'boy', and to 'Far is to near as there is to—— ' his response was 'office'. The only verbal analogy items on which he did make the right responses were ones that a child could answer by simply saying an associated word, without any genuinely analogous thinking being necessary, as in, for instance, 'Birds, fly; fish, *swim*' and 'Water, glass; coffee, *cup*'. In fact, Richard's answers to each of a variety of different verbal tests appeared to reflect associative responding of this primitive kind.

Richard was quite good at learning specific actions and memorizing particular items of written information. He could produce a learned sequence upon demand, although only in an automatic, parrot-like fashion. His behaviour was reported to have had something of the quality of a robot or computer routine, running faultlessly if correctly triggered, but rigid, stereotyped, and unadaptive. Thus, having been carefully trained to make appropriate social responses when he entered a room, Richard would utter stock greetings such as 'How are you, Dr G?'; or 'How is Mrs R?'. Quite often, the social response he chose to make would be one that was not at all suitable for the particular circumstances. For example, on leaving a room he was once observed to say, 'Goodbye, give me a kiss' to everyone in the room, including complete strangers. Adding to the oddity of his activities was the fact that his social remarks were not accompanied by the customary non-verbal gestures that most people make. Their absence contributed to the robot-like aspect of his behaviour.

The combination of an ability to remember lengthy written materials with a failure to have any real grasp of the meaningful content is illustrated by Richard's performance after he had successfully memorized Abraham Lincoln's Gettysburg Address. He could recite it all by heart, without a single error, but he could not give a sensible answer to the simple question, 'Who was Lincoln?'. Despite the fact that his school class had spent weeks studying a book about Lincoln's life, Richard's replies to questions about Lincoln, whenever not actually wrong, were trivial or superficial. When Richard was questioned about the content of a movie he had very recently watched, Chaplin's *The Great Dictator*, all he said was, 'It's about an airplane and a tank.'

Richard was totally defeated by any situation which required him to choose a plan of action or make a simple decision. If he was given precise instructions, he could cope with simple tasks like going to a shop, answering the telephone, or getting himself dressed or undressed, but if it was necessary for him to select what to wear, or choose between two items at the shop, or if an unexpected telephone call required him to decide on an answer, Richard could not deal with the situation at all. His day-to-day life was largely made up of carefully learned sequences of behaviour, such as taking milk and cookies at the instructed hour, putting his clothes on, and tying his shoelaces correctly. Richard performed these acts as fixed and unvarying ceremonies that left no room at all for flexibility. And his rigidity placed severe restrictions upon what he could do. For example, he had been taught to divide numbers and to do calculations that involved fractions, but if the stroke in a division sign or a fraction was not drawn at the exact angle to which he was accustomed, he would completely fail to recognize the sign.

In their investigation Scheerer, Rothmann and Goldstein sought to account for Richard's curious pattern of achievements and failures. Most people who have the language skills that are necessary for the memorizing and other word tasks at which Richard did so well are also able to understand and think about the content which language expresses: language and reasoning appear to be inseparable. But in a mentally handicapped person language skills may appear to be relatively isolated from other abilities, and restricted to utterances that are concrete and egocentric.

The absence of an ability to think and communicate at a level that is not tied to the literal meanings of each particular word precludes those kinds of thought that demand a metaphorical understanding of language or the capacity to detect symbolic and conceptual elements. Those test questions which require a person to give word definitions, detect similarities or differences between words, or supply opposites, all necessitate a degree of abstract reasoning. And as we have seen, Richard failed them completely.

A further consequence of Richard's lacking non-literal comprehension of language was that he had no idea of cause and effect. We take it for granted that everyone understands the concept of causation, to the extent that it is difficult to appreciate that a mentally retarded person may quite fail to realize that certain events can cause other things to happen. It is especially hard to accept that a capacity so fundamental as an understanding of the idea of cause and effect may be absent in an individual who is capable of the very impressive positive achievements exhibited by a retarded savant. Nevertheless, in Richard's case, it is clear that he had no understanding of causes at all. When he watched a conjuror performing, making items disappear and re-appear, Richard was bored and unimpressed. For him, there was no reason to notice anything at all strange or unexpected about the unlikely events that the conjuror caused to happen. The reason for Richard experiencing no surprise or wonder at the conjuror's acts was that in the absence of an understanding of cause and effect the tricks that were performed appeared to him to be no more and no less surprising than the routine happenings of everyday life.

At a later stage in Richard's life, his case came to the attention of another researcher, Louise LaFontaine. She interviewed him in 1967, and again in 1974. He was then forty-seven years of age. Richard lived in residential state schools until 1973, when he was transferred to a home which housed thirteen former state school residents. They worked for several hours each day in a nearby sheltered workshop. LaFontaine (1974) reported that Richard had made a satisfactory adjustment to the new environment and paid regular visits to his family: they had maintained close contact with him. On the occasion of the 1967 interview, LaFontaine found Richard somewhat withdrawn and remote, but she had more success in talking to him in 1974. At this time he not only told her that he remembered the previous visit, but he was able to recall the exact date, and he also recalled various details that she had told him in 1967, such as the birthdays of her children. LaFontaine tested Richard's abilities at calendar calculating, and she found that for dates between 1800 and 1985 he made seventeen correct responses out of eighteen. However, when she questioned him on dates between 1790 and 1800 Richard answered the questions incorrectly. He became so upset that LaFontaine decided that it would be wise to discontinue testing.

I have described Richard at some length, partly to give a fuller indication than a summary could provide of the manner in which a retarded savant's fragmentary achievements and disabilities may exist side by side. Although the investigations made relatively little progress towards explaining Richard's behaviour, they draw attention to an important defect which seems to run through many of his limitations: the apparent lack of an ability to think abstractly, or non-literally. One might be tempted to conclude that a deficit in abstract reasoning was *the* main cause of Richard's many symptoms of mental retardation. But cause and effect in human psychology are rarely simple or unidirectional.

AUTISM AND RETARDED SAVANTS

The different individuals who share the attributes of retarded savants form a highly varied group of people, but it would be not unreasonable to regard Richard as being as typical as any of them. Like him, most retarded savants are male and, in common with many savants, perhaps the majority, Richard could be described as being markedly 'autistic' in his personality and behaviour.

Autistic individuals usually appear to be aloof, isolated and withdrawn. They are poor at communicating with others, and may appear totally uninterested in other people. They seem to have great trouble understanding anything to do with social relationships. They may give the impression of living in a private and inaccessible dreamworld. Perceptual and cognitive impairments are thought to underly the observed disorders and behavioural abnormalities (Prior 1979). Most autistic children are mentally handicapped to some extent, but they may at the same time be highly talented, and in a number of ways they can be very different from other mentally handicapped people. The term was first used to describe people with these attributes by Leo Kanner, who borrowed it from Eugen Bleuler, a contemporary of Freud (Rimland 1964).

It is usual to give some emphasis to language deficiencies and to abnormalities in social behaviours when deciding whether or not it is appropriate to describe a child as being autistic. For example, Michael Rutter (1978) lists the four most important criteria as being, (1) onset prior to the age of thirty months; (2) impaired social development, which is out of line with the child's intellectual progress; (3) delayed and unusual language development; and (4) rigid or inflexible behaviour, demonstrated by resistance to change, abnormal preoccupations or stereotyped activities. Most experts agree that it is useful to make a distinction between autism and mental retardation, despite the fact that the majority of autistic children are mentally retarded. Rutter considers that autistic individuals have a defect in cognition that involves central coding processes and affects language abilities. In this respect, the defects that lead to a child being autistic may be more specific and less varied than the causes of mental retardation.

Underlying the failure of autistic children to experience genuine social relationships may be a total lack of awareness that other people are different from other objects in the world. It has been suggested that their thinking lacks

> a mechanism which underlies a crucial aspect of social skill, namely being able to conceive of mental states: that is, knowing that other people know, want, feel, or believe things; in short, having what Premack and Woodruff (1978) termed a 'theory of mind'. (Baron-Cohen, Leslie, and Frith 1985: 38)

Some researchers believe that particular neurological impairments underlie autism, although the exact nature, causes and location of the damage are not known (Leslie and Frith 1988). Hermelin and O'Connor (1970; see also Hermelin, 1976) have suggested that those aspects of cognitive coding which are most affected are the ones that are necessary for transforming information from one modality (auditory, tactile, visual or spatial) to another modality. When information is presented via a given modality, these children appear to be less capable than other children of responding in an alternative mode – for example, reading aloud letters that have been presented to them visually. Autistic children often seem to be happier with spatial rather than verbal tasks (Boygo and Ellis 1988, Waterhouse 1988).

It is important to emphasize that simply describing a child as autistic does not necessarily help us to explain the deficits and abnormalities that are observed. The term is little more than a descriptive label. Despite all the research many questions about the causes of autism remain unanswered, although it has been established that searching for one simple explanation or a single cause is unlikely to prove fruitful. Nevertheless, there are some interesting links between autistic behaviours and the achievements of retarded savants, and this fact could prove to be a useful aid to explanation. In a large sample of 5,400 autistic children, over 500 were found by one researcher, Bernard Rimland (1978) to have special abilities that warranted classification as idiots savants. However, these figures conflict with another estimate, by A. Lewis Hill (1977). He calculates that savants number only about 1 per 2,000 mentally retarded people. Since the incidence of autism amongst mental retardates is generally reckoned to be considerably higher than 1 in 200, the two sets of figures are definitely contradictory. To complicate things even further, yet another expert, Margot Prior (1979), asserts that idiot savant skills are just as rare among autistic people as they are among mentally handicapped individuals in general.

There are a number of possible reasons for the discrepancies in the measures of incidence. For instance, differences in the criteria used by researchers for classifying people as being idiots savants may be a contributing factor. Also, a selection bias might result if children from certain social classes are at the same time more likely than others to have the label 'autistic' applied to them and also more likely to have attention drawn to their special talents. Parental overestimates of the abilities of some autistic children can be yet another cause of bias, as Margot Prior points out. This could lead to the proportion of autistic children having savant skills being overestimated.

The extent to which it may be valuable to look for connections between savant skills and autism depends to some extent upon the degree to which the causes of autism are understood. About this matter there is considerable controversy. It is very unlikely that any single set of causes will account for all or even the majority of those individuals who have been classified as autistic. Nevertheless, some observations by Bernard Rimland suggest that searching for links with autism may eventually prove fruitful. Rimland notes that a number of writers have drawn attention to evidence indicating that autistic children are most deficient at those abilities which depend upon the left hemisphere of the brain. Functions that are considered to be largely controlled by the left hemisphere, including linguistic and sequential processes, are commonly impaired, but there is usually much less retardation of those functions that are attributed to the right hemisphere. However, to confuse matters, some of the skills displayed by retarded savants are ones which, at least in normal people, appear to be largely controlled by the left hemisphere. It is certainly possible that in certain idiots savants there is some imbalance or deficit in the manner in which the two brain hemispheres operate, but up to now the ideas that have been put forward concerning possible relationships between hemispheric localization and special skills have done little to extend our under-standing of retarded savants in general.

Rimland points out that amongst those children who are loosely described as being autistic, only about ten per cent meet the stricter criteria laid down by Kanner in the 1940s as being necessary for diagnosis as 'classical' cases of early infant autism. Among this smaller and somewhat rare group of individuals, Rimland notes that the incidence of retarded savant talents is considerably higher than it is in the broader autistic population. Rimland also states that those children diagnosed as being cases of classical autism 'almost invariably are the offspring of parents of exceptional intelligence' (Rimland 1978: 55). Also, in many of them there is strong evidence that a biochemical abnormality exists, involving an unusually high efflux of the neurotransmitter serotonin from the blood platelets (assessed by a radioactive tracer assay technique).

In discussing possible reasons for the fact that classically diagnosed autistic children are born to intelligent parents, Rimland draws attention to the observation that highly successful and intelligent people do share one characteristic with idiots savants. The shared attribute is that they have the ability to concentrate their attention on particular tasks, and sustain it over lengthy periods of time. Putting together his views and observations, Rimland concludes that some of the children who display retarded savant abilities are individuals in whom certain biochemical abnormalities are combined with a genetically transmitted predisposition towards high intelligence.

Rimland's contribution to the study of autism has undoubtedly been important but it is hard to assess the extent to which his views will further our understanding of retarded savants. One problem is that only a small proportion of those mentally handicapped people who display exceptional talents fit into the category of classical early infant autism. Apart from diagnostic reasons for saying this, there is the logical point that, whereas the parents of children with classical early infant autism are usually intelligent and well educated, the parental intelligence of the majority of retarded savants is not above average.

The identification of a biochemical abnormality involving high serotonin levels in some idiots savants is of great interest, yet there is no guarantee that it will open the way either to our being able to specify direct causes of the behavioural abnormalities or to the possibility of suggesting practical remedial steps. Discovering a relationship between physical and behavioural abnormalities has sometimes led researchers to conclude that there is simple cause-and-effect linkage between the two, but in fact that is rarely the case.

THE INCIDENCE OF SAVANT SKILLS

Just how rare are retarded savant skills? It has proved exceedingly difficult to estimate the proportion of retarded people who merit being classified as idiots savants. There are many problems. For example, if we start with an acceptable definition, such as 'a person of low general intelligence who possesses an unusually high degree of skill at some special task or tasks', it is quickly apparent that some important particulars remain undefined. How low does 'low' intelligence have to be, and at what point does the level of a skill become 'unusually high'? Even if firm objective criteria were to be established for a particular skill, there would remain the problem of comparing the degrees of exceptionality of individuals having different skills. And in addition to these unresolved questions, there are serious practical problems. For example, the fact that certain feats are more noticeable than others may influence the likelihood of a particular individual being classified as a savant. Consequently, the skills of those people who draw attention to themselves by performing unusual feats such as calendar calculating may be more likely to be noticed than, say, the memory skills of a very uncommunicative mentally handicapped person. Furthermore, there is the added difficulty that in order to assess the numbers of idiots savants it is necessary to gain the co-operation of the numerous administrators of the institutions where they reside.

In the face of all these difficulties, Hill (1977) has attempted to measure the incidence of idiot savant abilities in the United States population of institutionalized mentally handicapped people. He wrote to a total of 300 facilities for the mentally handicapped, and received responses from a third of them. From the reports he was sent he calculated that around 0.06 per cent of the retarded population in public residential facilities could be classified as being savants; that is, roughly 1 out of every 2,000 mentally retarded residents. But Hill stresses that this estimate should be regarded with considerable caution, owing to possible bias in the sample, in addition to all the other difficulties listed above.

HARRIET

For a second biographical account of the life and personality of a retarded savant, I describe a mentally retarded woman, named Harriet. Female savants are certainly less numerous than male savants, but despite the (unsubstantiated) assertion by some authors that retarded savants are much rarer among women than men, the actual difference in incidence is not greatly more than the statistics for sex differences in the numbers of mentally retarded people would lead on to expect. As you will discover, there are some points of similarity in the lives and accomplishments of Harriet and Richard, but there are vast differences as well. For example, the roles played by the two mothers contrast sharply, and whilst Richard might fairly have been described as an autistic child, that term could not be applied to Harriet.

Harriet's family background was very different from that of Richard. No member of Harriet's family gave her anything like the degree of care and attention that Richard received from his devoted mother. Harriet's mother, a domineering and rather selfish Italian-American woman who made a living by teaching singing, gave birth to seven children. Harriet, who was born and grew up in Boston, Massachusetts, was the sixth. As an adult, although she was considered to be mentally retarded, Harriet managed to hold a job as a kitchen assistant for over twenty years. She prepared the salads in a Jewish hospital, where she was regarded as a conscientious and reliable worker who never missed a single day's work until she broke her ankle about a year prior to her admission to Boston State Hospital in 1956, at the age of forty, in a very confused and deluded state. It was at that point that David Viscott, a Boston psychiatrist, became interested in Harriet's case, and he wrote an account of her life and achievements (Viscott 1970).

One month before Harriet was born her mother had a severe fright when her eldest daughter narrowly evaded a serious accident. The mother became convinced that her new child would be defective, and after Harriet's birth she decided to keep the baby with her for protection at all times in the studio where she earned a living by giving music lessons. Music thus became an almost constant element in Harriet's early environment. Her mother soon noticed that on the very rare occasions when Harriet cried, the sound of the piano would calm her.

As an infant, Harriet seems to have received very little maternal attention while the music lessons were in progress. Since the other children in the family were not allowed into the studio, social contacts in Harriet's early years must have been minimal. To make things worse, Harriet's mother spent so much of her time teaching pupils that the other children saw very little of her, and resenting what appeared to them to be Harriet's privileged position in the family, they took to punishing and tormenting the new baby. The discovery that this was happening led in turn to the mother increasing Harriet's isolation from her brothers and sisters, in an effort to protect the child from being harmed. Consequently, ignored by her mother for long periods of time, and deprived of the stimulation that is normally

31

provided by other family contacts, Harriet spent her early years in a state of unusual isolation. Like many deprived infants she began to engage in odd rocking and head-banging activities. These served to confirm her mother's suspicion that the child was defective.

The first indication that Harriet might possess some special abilities came in her eighth month. Harriet's father, hearing musical noises coming from the studio noticed that,

> She was lying on her back in her crib and humming in perfect pitch, tempo and phrasing the 'Caro Nome' from *Rigoletto*, a popular aria of the mother's students. She also sang their vocalises, their exercises, in all keys, major and minor, and with the proper accents, phrasing and pitch. (Viscott 1970: 498)

From this point onwards, Harriet's mother was certain that her daughter was unique. She now began to think that Harriet, far from being defective, was especially talented, doubtless as a result of inheriting the musical talents that were in the maternal blood. But Harriet continued to be isolated from social contact and stimulation, music excepted. No one played with her. She rarely cried and never smiled, and her head-banging and rocking increased.

Two years after Harriet's birth her mother's routine was disrupted through illness following the birth of another daughter, who was born with a deformed foot. At last Harriet began to experience something like normal family life; but she was ill-prepared for it and she was not an easy child. Much of her time was spent breaking anything she could find. Her brothers and sisters often teased her, and she retaliated by destroying their toys and tormenting their pets. At this period of her life she did not talk at all despite her mother's efforts to make her communicate. Not until she was nine years old did she learn to speak normally and become properly toilet trained.

Where music was concerned, however, the story of Harriet's progress was remarkably different. When she was two her banging and hitting motions were seen to follow some kind of rhythmic tempo, and it was clear that she loved to make noises. If one of her mother's pupils produced a note that was off pitch Harriet would yelp as if it had caused her real pain. On one occasion, when a student repeatedly failed to sing a high note correctly, Harriet ran at him and tried to push him out of the house. The sound of someone striking the notes of a poorly tuned piano caused her anguish. Once, after her brother had teased her by doing so, she physically attacked the piano, ripping out the offending key and hammer.

When she was three, Harriet would sit and watch her eldest sister practise at the piano, and she began to play the instrument herself, always hitting the right note. Without having any lessons she quickly learned to play all the other musical instruments she could find in the house, including a violin, a trumpet, a clarinet and a French horn. By four years of age she could play all the arias sung by her mother's pupils, with correct fingering and harmony. By seven she could accompany all the pupils, and she played the piano and the violin better than any of her brothers and sisters.

At around this time, with Harriet's musical talents beginning to become well known in the neighbourhood, it appears that some kind of expert came to see her. He was described by Harriet's mother as 'a philosopher in psychology'. This man (whoever he was) pronounced Harriet to be a genius. Yet his proposal that Harriet be taken away for a year to receive special musical training was successfully resisted by Harriet's father, who was firmly convinced that a woman's place was in the home.

Much of Harriet's behaviour remained wild and uncontrollable. Her torturing of the family pets culminated in two cats being killed. But in addition to her musical ability, she began to display another remarkable talent – for memorization. Harriet would often go with her father to the garage where he worked as an automobile mechanic, and despite her poor speech she quickly learned the names for all the different makes and models of cars. She was soon able to identify all the different parts by the correct name. Furthermore, she could remember every single one of the weather reports she had heard on the radio: on being told a date by someone in her family she would immediately recite the appropriate report. She could also recall on request any of about three hundred telephone numbers that had been told to her by her relations or by students and other people who visited the house. Once, her father read to her the first three pages of the Greater Boston Telephone Directory. For several years afterwards Harriet could remember any of these numbers on demand. She also showed great interest in calendars.

At the age of nine Harriet started to attend school, but although she was placed in a special class it was not a success and she stayed for only two months. She returned to school again at eleven, and learned to read and draw by the time she left at sixteen. At eighteen, with the help of her deformed younger sister Mary, she was given the job which she was to keep until she was forty. For the first six months Mary helped with her training, until a rigid, unvarying routine had been acquired, and Harriet was able to manage on her own. As a worker, she was cheerful, uncomplaining and always reliable. Half of the spare money from her earnings regularly went into the bank, and the remainder was spent on recordings of classical music. Her life in the succeeding years followed a fixed pattern and was uneventful. She did her work at the hospital, and at home she looked after many of the cooking, cleaning and shopping jobs. She continued to accompany her mother's pupils. In her leisure time Harriet listened to music.

One Christmas day, when she was in her thirties, for the first time in her life she told her family about a dream, in which she saw her father die. For some time he had been suffering from heart disease. Just before the Christmas dinner he actually died. The family were horrified by Harriet's apparent lack of distress. They reported that she did not cry at all, and sat down alone to eat just after the body had been carried out.

David Viscott, whose published description of Harriet's early years I have summarized, tested Harriet when he first encountered her at Boston State Hospital. Her IQ on the Weschler scale was 73, her performance being markedly lower on verbal than on non-verbal items. She did well on some memory tests, but her general knowledge was highly uneven: for instance, she believed that there were forty-eight weeks in a year and ten feet in a yard.

In common with Leonard/Lionel, and Richard, and the majority of mentally handicapped people, Harriet was greatly impaired in the ability to reason abstractly. When she was asked to state how certain items were similar to each other she showed the same inability to introduce abstract concepts and metaphorical ideas that was noticed in Richard's case. For example, asked how a nickel was like a dime, Harriet could only reply, 'a nickel is a nickel and a dime is a dime' despite all that Viscott could do to coax her into noticing any of their shared attributes, such as roundness, metallic composition or monetary functions. Like Richard, Harriet was also very poor at giving word definitions and at perceiving the non-literal meanings of metaphors and understanding proverbs. But her performance at motor skills and visual patterns involving patterns, figures, and a knowledge of spatial orientation was considerably better than Richard's.

Viscott discovered that Harriet was a competent calendar calculator. She could provide the correct day of the week for any date between 1925 and 1970. It became clear to Viscott that Harriet could remember several hundred particular days, and that these served her as a source of anchor dates that could be used for calculating other days. He also noticed that far more errors than usual were made on those questions that referred to dates in the year in which her father had died.

Viscott's questioning revealed that Harriet possessed a fund of musical knowledge that he described as 'breathtaking'. In music, moreover, Harriet gave evidence of having a power for abstraction and the ability to experience feelings, two qualities that appeared to be absent from other spheres of her life. In this respect Harriet was not unlike Leonard/Lionel. It became apparent that Harriet could identify all the symphonic music that is played at all regularly. She could also provide information about the composer of any piece of music, and she could state the date of first performance and give the correct key and opus number. She was especially well informed about opera, her knowledge extending to numerous works of lesser-known composers. It emerged that for the past twenty years Harriet had attended every concert in the Saturday Evening series given by the Boston Symphony Orchestra. She was able to recall details of each single performance and could say what was played and who conducted, and she had a large store of detailed information about the life, musical experience, qualifications and background of every single member of the entire orchestra. Like Leonard/Lionel, with whom her case has a number of interesting similarities, she also possessed a huge quantity of biographical knowledge about the lives of composers and musical performers.

Harriet's own ability as a musical performer was extremely impressive. Anyone who knows the struggle that learning music can involve will wonder at her facility. Having absolute pitch enabled her to recognize the pitch of any kind of sound, not only music notes. If a four-note chord was held on the piano for just half a second she could name every one of the component notes. She could also state the key and mode of any chord, and she could name each of two random notes struck simultaneously. When she played an orchestral work on the piano she would spontaneously fill in parts from the full orchestral version that did not appear in her piano score. When playing a transcribed version of a part that originated with a different instrument she would carefully imitate the instrument's tone and phrasing.

She transcribed from memory. She could make difficult changes of key in the middle of playing a piece of music. And whenever Harriet played or listened to music her face was seen to display feelings and emotions that never appeared in any of her other activities.

Contrasting with the rigidity and passivity that marked Harriet's non-musical life, her activities as a musician were full of expressive and improvisational features. Even her language, when she was talking about music, often included words that referred to feelings, such as sweet, lovely, sad, scary and frightening. When she played operatic music she was able to communicate both in words and in her playing the emotions experienced by the characters. She could give detailed descriptions of the plots of operas and the motives of the characters. In contrast to Leonard/Lionel, Harriet's love of music was not limited to the classical repertoire: she also enjoyed rock, jazz and popular music.

From the description of Harriet it is clear that as well as sharing a number of attributes with Leonard/Lionel she was also similar to Richard in some respects. Both of them liked music, and both had some calendar skills. But two aspects of her life sharply contrasted with Richard's, quite apart from the differences in the form of their particular talents. First, whereas knowing about Richard's family and early background gives virtually no clues that might help us to account for his handicaps, some features of Harriet's early life do hint at possible causes. Her mother's difficulties in accepting the child, and the absence of contact and attention from other people, may well have influenced Harriet's psychological development. Viscott writes of Harriet's talent for music being 'forced to carry not merely her feelings but her language as well' (Viscott 1970: 510). This view may appear exaggerated but it is certainly true that, whereas the early world of most young children is one that is filled with language and social acts, for Harriet music seems to have been the one permanent feature of everyday life and the one to which she seems to have enjoyed giving attention. Viscott also draws attention to the ties between her musical ability and her relationship with her mother. This relationship was certainly a very unusual one, and may well have contributed to some of Harriet's problems.

The second important difference between Richard and Harriet is that while Richard's lack of an ability to think abstractly appears to have extended to every aspect of mental life, this was not true of Harriet. In the sphere of music the evidence of her achievements firmly suggests that she could reason abstractly, and that unlike Richard she also had the capacity to incorporate emotional and affective elements into her mental life. After reading Richard's case history on its own one might be tempted to conclude that lack of abstract thought is *the* basic cause of the handicaps suffered by retarded savants. But the account of Harriet, in whom a failure to think abstractly in most areas of experience was apparently combined with a much richer mental life in one particular sphere, music, underlines the futility of trying to explain the deficits in terms of any one simple factor.

Further comparisons between pairs of retarded savants would reveal further similarities between them and some additional differences as well. Harriet and Leonard/Lionel are by no means the only reported cases of excellent musicianship in mentally retarded individuals. (See, for example, Charness et al. 1988, Lucci et al. 1988, Miller 1987, Sloboda et al. 1985 and Treffert 1989.) But by no means all retarded savants have included music among their achievements: in fact the majority has not. In some instances it appears very probable that the nature of a retarded person's talents has been strongly influenced by the individual's particular environment. This definitely seems to have been true for Harriet, but it was not so obviously the case for Richard. Even in Harriet, while the particular circumstances of her life almost certainly did have an influence on her acquisition of musical abilities, it is not easy to detect clear links between her early environment and certain of her other skills, such as calendar calculating. We ought to be prepared for the possibility that whereas in some people the factors that cause a particular talent to bloom may be directly related to the nature and causes of a person's retardation, in others the determinants of a particular talent may be entirely unrelated to the exact form and nature of mental handicap.

The descriptions of Richard and Harriet have helped to clarify some of the issues raised in Chapter 1. In each of these two cases, and also in that of Leonard/Lionel, it is clear that their mental handicap was real enough: the low levels of competence outside their areas of special accomplishments cannot be dismissed as being either illusory or caused by a primarily social or communicative handicap. It is also clear from all three cases that the special skills were genuinely remarkable ones, although perhaps less so in Richard than in the other individuals. It would be absurd to suggest that any normal individual who decided to specialize in music could match either Harriet's or Leonard/Lionel's musical accomplishments.

The accounts of Richard and Harriet also illustrate the fact that individual retarded savants differ very markedly in their personalities. Richard's developmental history is in some respects typical of autistic childhoods (although it is arguable whether any strictly 'typical' autistic child exists). Certain of Harriet's personality characteristics are ones that are often associated with autism, but in all likelihood she was no more autistic than the majority of people with an equivalent degree of mental handicap.

As was remarked in Chapter 1, retarded savants are diverse in many ways, including the degree of their retardation. Some have a level of mental functioning that is considerably lower than either Richard or Harriet. In fact, Harriet's level of intelligence would place her, in general ability, towards the upper end of the distribution of the individuals who have been labelled as idiots savants. This raises two interesting questions. First, how should we describe the many people who are average or slightly below average in general intelligence but who possess particular mental skills that reach extremely high standards? Such people certainly do exist, perhaps the most striking among them being the individuals who perform feats of memory or mental calculations. In a number of specializations, including mathematics, chess-playing and music, there are people who combine outstanding competence in their chosen field with a level of ability to perform other intellectual tasks that is no more than average. There is no clear line dividing such individuals from the most intelligent retarded savants. Indeed, although it is those who combine retardation with special abilities who strike our attention as being most obviously remarkable, the existence of people of normal intelligence who exhibit vast differences in the levels at which they function within different intellectual fields is no less deserving of attention, and equally challenging to accepted wisdom concerning the (apparently) unitary and centralized nature of human intelligence.

The second question is even more important and is one to which we will return in later chapters. It asks whether or not individuals in whom levels of expertise in different spheres of life differ as sharply as they do in retarded savants are actually any less frequent among people who are not mentally handicapped than among the retarded population from which the reported cases of retarded savants have been taken. In other words, might not the fragmentariness of the abilities that seize our attention when we observe a retarded savant, and the noticeably extreme divergence between the levels of one individual's performance at different mental tasks, be equally likely to occur in ordinary people who are not mentally retarded?

Marked variability within an individual's pattern of abilities is especially easy to notice in people who are mentally handicapped. In them, special skills are thrown into sharp relief by the low level of mental functioning in most other areas. But it is by no means inconceivable that the size of the differences between the levels of an individual's skills is in reality no larger in retarded savants than in equally frequent instances of non-retarded people. In practice, unfortunately, it would not be at all easy to do the measuring and counting exercises necessary for comparing within-individual divergence in normal and mentally handicapped populations. As I pointed out earlier in this chapter, severe obstacles are encountered when one tries to assess the incidence of retarded savants among mentally handicapped people: any attempt to estimate the numbers of ordinary people having skills that demand a degree of mental ability that contrasts with levels of competence in other areas would meet with even greater difficulties.

There is one fairly compelling reason for believing that specialized skills in people of broadly normal ability are at least unlikely to be quite so fragmentary and out of line with a person's average level of mental functioning as they are in mentally retarded savants. This reason is that, generally speaking, there is a greater degree of transfer between learned abilities in people of normal intelligence, compared with mentally handicapped individuals, and the former are better at applying learned skills in new situations and altered circumstances, and modifying existing abilities in order to deal with new tasks. Mentally handicapped learners are almost always rather poor at applying their skills to new circumstances: abilities may be context-bound to an extreme degree. For instance, there is the case of a mentally retarded man who had been carefully trained to work with a highly complex piece of industrial machinery (Zigler and Seitz, 1982). So long as the conditions in which he was required to work were identical to those in which he had learned to work the machine his performance was excellent. However, if the workshop director altered the conditions slightly by turning the machine to face a different direction, the man became totally incapable of operating it.

An intelligent person's abilities are generally less rigidly bound to particular circumstances, and more accessible. However, to present a stark contrast in which the skills of retarded savants are regarded as fixed and fragmentary, inflexible and narrowly specialized, whilst a normal person's abilities are seen to be adaptable, flexible, generalizable, and applicable and transferable to all kinds of new circumstances would be quite unrealistic. Even in highly intelligent individuals, achievements are often bound to particular contexts to a surprising degree, and there is often a remarkable absence of ability to apply existing skills to new circumstances in which they could be useful. Transfer may be highly restricted, and there often appears to be little co-ordination between different skills. Therefore, although retarded savants may differ from other people in the size of the gap between their levels of ability at different tasks, the difference, if it exists, is only a relative one. And by drawing attention to the fragmentariness of special skills in certain unusual individuals, case histories of idiots savants have performed the unanticipated service of alerting us to the fact that people of any level of ability may have skills that are highly specialized, fragmentary, and autonomous, a fact that may force us to rethink some of our ideas about the governing and co-ordinating functions of human intelligence.

A final point for the present chapter. Some retarded savants suffer from particular physical deficits such as deafness or blindness, as well as being mentally handicapped. (In many cases, such extra handicaps may have contributed to mental retardation, of course.) Knowing about the sensory handicaps of particular individuals would be very useful when one is trying to assess the merits of assertions that have been put forward as general explanations. For example, a theory that all retarded savants who can perform a certain skill do so by making use of mental imagery becomes very hard to maintain after we have encountered the same skill in a mentally handicapped person who is congenitally blind.

The major concern of this chapter has been to present fairly detailed descriptions of the lives of just two individuals amongst the numerous people who have been classified as being retarded savants. In the following chapters there will be further descriptions of the skills of particular retarded savants, but increasing attention will also be given to efforts to explain how and why the various feats are achieved, typically in unlikely circumstances, and to understand how it is that certain people can be simultaneously retarded and capable of remarkable achievements. Chapter 3 investigates the memory skills of mentally handicapped savants. Many of the most striking feats are essentially feats of memory, and the ones that are not nearly always depend upon memorization to a considerable extent.

Chapter Three

EXPLAINING FEATS OF MEMORY

Almost all the skills of retarded savants make heavy demands on memory. Numerous feats of remembering as such have been recorded, and memory also plays a big role in the other achievements, including those of mental arithmetic, calendar calculating, and even musical abilities.

A catalogue of all the different kinds of information which retarded savants have taken it upon themselves to remember would contain a bewildering variety of entries, including names and dates of many kinds, addresses, zip codes, area codes and telephone numbers, many types of population statistics, geographical information, timetables, poetry, stories (recalled word for word), licence numbers, menus, road maps, date-based information about family events, weather reports, news items, locomotive engine numbers and freight train car numbers, stations on railways routes, songs, word spellings, (backwards as well as forwards), birthdays, street sequences, word-by-word records of conversations, television and film scripts, sporting events and statistics, and astronomical information.

Quite often, the information that is recalled in such impressive detail is highly specific in nature and apparently unrelated to any of the individual's other interests or practical concerns. It is hard to understand how certain of the topics could ever capture someone's attention. For instance, one autistic seven-year-old remembered the English and Latin names of eighteen different varieties of deer, despite the fact that he was quite ignorant of the Latin language and would not have recognized a single one of the animals if it had presented itself in front of him.

In other instances, the memory abilities do make an essential contribution to mental activities. In common with calendar calculating skills (which are examined in Chapter 5), feats of mental arithmetic depend especially heavily on remembering. Before the days of electronic calculators prodigious feats of 'lightning' calculating used to attract a great deal of public attention, especially in the eighteenth and nineteenth centuries. Spectators would pay to watch and marvel at the most remarkable feats. These included calculating how many times a coach wheel measuring five feet ten inches in circumference would revolve in running 800 million miles, or the distance from a star to the earth, if light takes six years and four months to do the journey – assuming that light takes eight minutes to travel the 98 million miles from the sun to the earth, or how many cubic inches there are in a right-angled block of stone 23,145,789 yards long, 5,642,732 yards wide, and 54,965 yards thick, and finding the cube root of 268,336,125 and the square root of 119,550,669,121.

It must be said that the very best lightning calculators have been individuals who were not mentally retarded, but substantial numbers of retarded savants have displayed calculating skills that far outstrip their own achievements at any other tasks, and a few of them have mastered feats that are almost as impressive as those of the most intelligent lightening calculators. As well as the mental calculations that were described in Chapter 1, retarded individuals have proved capable of such difficult feats as being able to state the cube root of any six-digit number within six seconds.

The chief aim of the present chapter is to explain how mentally retarded savants are able to achieve their memory feats. A number of questions is addressed. Do retarded savants have memory skills that are 'special' and quite distinct from those of other people? In order to perform memory feats is it necessary to have a definite intention to do so? How are savants' achievements affected by their knowledge and interests? Do memory tasks provide a way for certain individuals to avoid events and thoughts that are threatening or unpleasant? What are the rewards for undertaking mammoth feats of memory? Can special memory feats actually cause or contribute to mental retardation? Are certain feats easier for mentally retarded individuals than for other people, and does retardation bring other advantages for the performance of memory tasks? Are some retarded individuals capable of achievements that would be quite impossible for people of average intelligence? Is it true that retarded savants are incapable of abstract thought?

DO RETARDED SAVANTS HAVE SPECIAL MEMORY ABILITIES?

First of all, consider two alternative possibilities. The first is that retarded savants possess memory systems that are in some fundamental way 'special', and different from the memories of ordinary people (O'Connor and Hermelin 1989). The second possibility is that the operation of memory in normal individuals and retarded savants is essentially similar. In the latter case, it would follow that when savants remember things especially well they do so for much the same reasons as the ones that account for some ordinary people being extraordinarily successful at certain memory tasks.

Do retarded savants have memory skills which are quite unlike those of ordinary people? Except in a few rare cases they probably do not. Whenever their memory abilities have been assessed by the use of standard mental tests, the scores have tended to be somewhat higher than those on items assessing other abilities, but not greatly so, and markedly lower than the scores gained by people of normal intelligence. A fairly typical case is that of a seven-year-old American boy who could state the name and the nearest neighbour of most American states and foreign countries and was able to recite countless addresses, telephone numbers and other lists of detailed information, although his IQ was only 37 and his mental age was two years and six months. But his performance on memory tests only equalled that of an average four-year-old (Goodman 1972). Even allowing for the fact that test situations rarely bring out the best in mentally retarded people, who may be confused by the unfamiliarity of the circumstances and lack the competitiveness that doing well at tests depends upon, there is no reason to suppose that the majority of retarded savants have fundamentally superior memory skills. To account for their striking feats of remembering we need to look elsewhere.

Yet there are some exceptions. A few cases have come to light of individuals who seem to have been able to reproduce large bodies of data to which they have been only briefly exposed. These people have often been mentally handicapped, but not always, and some of them have been autistic, psychotic, or disturbed in some other way. For example, Albert Cain (1969) reported the case of a six-and-a-half-year-old autistic girl who would never look at other people, had no communicative use of language, seemed not to hear at all and was entirely passive and apparently aimless. Nevertheless, he noted:

But Millie has a phenomenal memory. She repeats verbatim (typically *not* upon request) lengthy conversations or radio or TV material, often heard years before. She accurately reads and reproduces (including the spelling) virtually any word she has seen even once, including words many years beyond her age level, and quickly corrects others' misspellings of such words. (Cain 1969: 139)

The description of Millie appears to lend support to the view that there are a few remarkable individuals who possess what might be called 'photographic' memory, in which the individual appears to register a literal copy of something he or she perceives, following one brief exposure. If this phenomenon does exist, it may have something in common with the ability possessed by perhaps one young child in every twenty (and a larger proportion of mentally handicapped children) to form what are known as 'eidetic' visual memory images (see Chapter 6), that sometimes appear to facilitate recall of literal details from recently seen pictures.

Cases such as Millie's show that we cannot rule out the possibility that a few retarded savants may have possessed memory skills that are quite distinct from those of other people. But much of the evidence to support this possibility is only anecdotal, and possibly unreliable. For instance, one description that appears to demonstrate quite extraordinary memory powers in an idiot savant appears in the case history of Harriet, who we discussed in the previous chapter. According to the report, when Harriet was about seven

her father read the first three pages of the Greater Boston Telephone Directory to her and for several years she could give any number of these pages on request. (Viscott 1970: 501)

An account such as this one does seem to confirm the existence of some kind of automatic registration process, whereby large amounts of newly perceived information are instantly and permanently stored in memory. But like most anecdotal descriptions it is reported at second hand; and some aspects of it cannot be verified. All we have to go on is Viscott's description of an account by Harriet's father of events that were said to have occurred over thirty years previously.

To be entirely convincing, evidence in support of the claim that there exist memory capacities that are fundamentally different from those of ordinary individuals would have to be collected under closely controlled conditions, in which the amount of exposure to the information could be manipulated, and recall carefully measured. In fact, whenever it has been possible to test subjects under such carefully controlled conditions the observed patterns of performance at memory tasks have failed to provide any firm evidence to support the assertion that certain individuals can immediately and permanently register large quantities of information in memory. Accurate memory for substantial amounts of information has only been observed when there has been an opportunity for the individual to study the information fairly carefully. It is also significant that examinations of the scores gained by retarded savants on the memory tasks in intelligence tests have always failed to reveal any evidence of abnormally accurate remembering. Furthermore, savant memory abilities are invariably restricted to certain kinds of information: there is no superior general capacity that produces elevated recall in each and every circumstance.

It remains conceivable that Millie, Harriet and a few other individuals might have possessed memory capabilities that were quite unlike those of ordinary people. Yet the chances are that the majority of retarded savants who remember certain items with remarkable accuracy do so for much the same reasons as other people sometimes do. The achievements are none the less remarkable, and explaining them is a formidable challenge. But in searching for clues we may do well to start by examining the causes of accurate remembering in the everyday lives of ordinary people.

IS AN INTENTION TO REMEMBER ESSENTIAL?

How is it possible for mentally retarded individuals to remember large amounts of information? And how do they do it? In trying to understand how and why it is that comparatively large numbers of retarded savants have been so successful at memory tasks we might start by asking ourselves why we find this fact so surprising.

We tend to assume that in order to retain a substantial amount of data in memory it is necessary to have a definite intention to do so. For instance, if asked to specify the factors that influence the likelihood of someone memorizing a verse of poetry, most adults would emphasize the importance of the person intending to memorize, and making a deliberate effort to do so, closely attending to the task and concentrating on the words to be remembered. By this reckoning the really

45

effective learner is likely to be a person who carefully studies the material.

But none of these activities is one at which people who are mentally handicapped can be expected to shine. Although the belief that all mentally retarded people are impulsive and unable to sustain concentration is certainly unjustified (and retarded savants can concentrate remarkably well), it is true to say that the sequence of events in which a definite intention to memorize is effectively transformed into deliberate study activities necessitates a degree of self-awareness and sophistication that many retarded savants do not possess. Such people are rarely capable of undertaking carefully organized plans of study. But if they are not, how can they possibly be capable of extraordinary memory feats?

The answer to this question is that, despite appearances, successful remembering does *not* depend upon someone setting out with a deliberate intention to remember. What *is* essential is that the individual gives close attention to the material. It is certainly helpful to have an intention and undertake planned study activities, because these help a person to sustain concentration, but neither intentionality nor deliberate studying is indispensible.

By and large, retarded savants remember things for roughly the same reasons that ordinary people sometimes remember well: items are retained in memory because they have received sustained and concentrated attention. And savants, like people of normal intelligence, are most likely to keep on concentrating on something if they find it especially interesting. What matters is that, for one reason or another, the information gains a person's close attention. If that person is sufficiently interested in something, the chances are that he or she will pay it sustained attention. This will result in quantities of information being remembered, despite the absence of any plan or intention to learn. Admittedly, many of the items that retarded savants memorize – zip codes, telephone numbers, and so on – are ones that a normal person would find less than enthralling; but that is not important. What is vital is that the attention of a savant is engaged, as it sometimes is for hours at a stretch. A mentally handicapped calendar calculator may be preoccupied with calendar dates for most of his waking time. The interests of such individuals are very different from those of ordinary people. Savants are extraordinary in *what* they remember, but not in *how* they remember.

Findings obtained from psychological research give ample support for the assertion that sustained attention leads to remembering even in the absence of any definite intention to remember. The point emerges especially clearly from a series of experiments conducted by Fergus Craik and Endel Tulving (1975). Some students (who served as subjects in the study) answered a sequence of questions, each of which asked about a word that was about to be shown, for a brief period of a second or less. After seeing the word, a subject had to write down the answer to the preceding question. For instance, the question might be, 'Does it rhyme with STONE?' If the word that then appeared was RONE the subject would answer 'Yes'. In a typical experiment a particular word could be coupled with any of three kinds of question. Some questions concerned the meaning of the subsequent word (e.g., 'Is it an animal?'), others asked about the sound (e.g., 'Does it rhyme with LEMON?'); and the third kind of question queried the visual appearance of the word (e.g., 'Is it in capital letters?').

The main finding of the experiments was that the likelihood of any word item being remembered was very strongly influenced by the form of question that had preceded it. In one study, for example, seventy-two per cent of the words that had been preceded by a question about the word's meaning were correctly recognized, compared with forty-six per cent of the words that followed a question about the sound, and only twenty-six per cent of those words that were coupled with a question that asked about its physical structure (the type-case of the letters). In short, having to attend to the meaning of an item that was being perceived led to a very substantial increase in the likelihood of that item being recalled, even in the absence of any intention to remember the words. Since in all three conditions exactly the same words were shown for identical amounts of time, the only possible explanation for the large differences in memory of the words lies in the different kinds of mental activities the subjects had to undertake (in order to answer the preceding question) as each word was perceived. That is, the nature of the cognitive processing that took place when a person saw a word item determined whether or not that item would be remembered.

Another experiment directly addressed the question of whether or not having an intention to remember has an effect on remembering. We know that intending to recall something may encourage us to attend to it more closely or to process it more carefully. But does an intention or a desire to remember words exert an influence over and above that of the differences in the mental processing (following the different kinds of questions) that occurs at the time the words are perceived? Perhaps surprisingly, the answer provided by the experimental findings was a definite 'No'. The participants' intention to remember was manipulated in the experiment by offering them incentives, in the form of money rewards, for every word they recognized correctly. The design of the study made it possible to measure the separate effects of two possible influences upon remembering: first, the kind of perceptual processing activity (determined by the form of question preceding each word) and, second, the subject's intention to remember (determined by the level of the financial incentive). The results of the experiment were unambiguous. The type of question asked had the same large influence that was observed in the study we have already described, but manipulating the intention to remember by varying the incentive had no effect at all on the subjects' memory for the words. In short, a research study that was designed in a way that ensured that the possible effects of intentionality and perceptual processing were kept separate found the influence on learning of having an intention to learn to be absolutely nil. Why, then, does intending to learn or remember something have a practical influence in everyday circumstances? In all probability, simply because one's intentions may affect the way in which information is perceived and attended to.

A moment's reflection reminds us that daily life contains many instances of accurate remembering in the absence of any deliberate intention to remember, let alone engaging in study. So long as someone is sufficiently interested in a topic to give it careful attention, remembering will result, even if there is not the slightest intention to memorize anything. Many ordinary people know the words of numerous songs, even if they have made no effort to learn them. And evey week in Britain during the soccer season millions of football enthusiasts can remember the weekend match scores of many teams in the English and Scottish football leagues. Serious fans do not have to make any deliberate attempt to memorize this information: after listening to the football results they remember a large proportion of the scores obtained in each of the sixty-four Saturday matches in the major leagues. Followers of other sports are equally good at recalling information about their own particular interests.

As a general rule, whenever people are interested enough in something to give it their enthusiastic attention, they find themselves able, without really trying, to remember striking numbers of detailed facts. It follows that there is no reason to assume that a retarded savant's success at remembering large bodies of information has to depend upon that person having engaged in the same kinds of deliberate and intentional activities that we would observe in a student who is studying for an examination. So long as there is enough interest to maintain close attention, considerable remembering takes place even in the absence of any deliberate memorizing.

That is not to say that retarded savants never intend to memorize, or never deliberately study things in an effort to remember. The point is simply that neither of these if essential for memorizing. In fact, there are certain cases in which retarded savants have been known to engage in study activities of one kind or another. For example, the man who recalled large amounts of detailed information about the railways in the region where he lived (according to the report made by Hiram Byrd in 1920) kept a notebook containing numerous names and numbers. Describing the notebook, Byrd records,

> Then comes a page with the following words on it: 'Engine Number is 1746 Run from Frogmoor to Mounds. Engine Number is 795 919 914 906 851 945 887 Run from Water Valley to Frogmoor 1 Miles to Jackson.' Given a start on this page, he reels off everything on it. Then comes another page which starts: 'Northern Line Passenger Engine Number is 1140 1139 1008 1051 1108 1065 1080 1141. Run from Champaign to Centralia 130 Miles Illinois Division Champaign district.
>
> He can repeat this page if given three or four words at the start. Several other pages of like matter follow, all of which he can repeat when given a start. Only the last page he can't repeat — it is too new. He has not committed it to memory yet. All this explains his passion for meeting the trains. It also explains that his method is one of committing to memory. (Byrd 1920: 206)

Again, the authors of a report on an eleven-year-old mildly retarded boy also draw attention to his studying activities. The boy seemed to have 'an unending supply of unconnected information', and his special skills included the ability to do mental arithmetic calculations at lightning speed. Apparently,

> Throughout his school career he was a great nuisance as he would often wander around or away from the classroom. At home he was considered odd by his siblings and spent most of his time sitting alone with dictionaries or encyclopedias repeating over and over

to himself the items he had read. He went around the house closing doors, arranging furniture in an orderly fashion, and putting everything back in its proper place. (Nurcombe and Parker 1964: 473)

KNOWING AND REMEMBERING

In retarded savants and people of normal intelligence alike, a number of influences can affect the likelihood of events being retained in memory. One of the most important factors is the extent to which the individual is already knowledgeable about whatever is being attended to: the ability to remember new information is affected by what one already knows concerning the topic in question. People are particularly successful at remembering information about things that are highly familiar and meaningful. Consequently it is found, for instance, that those individuals who are the most successful at remembering the scores of soccer matches are the people with the greatest amount of general knowledge about soccer (Morris *et al.* 1981). Familiarity is so important, in fact, that it can more than wipe out the usual advantage which adults have at memory tasks, compared with young children. Thus Michelene Chi (1978) found that ten-year-olds who were good at chess were much more successful at remembering the positions of chess pieces on the board than adults who knew the rules of chess but were less knowledgeable about the game. In retarded savants, the fact that their interests tend to be narrower, less wide-ranging and more specialized than those of highly intelligent individuals, can bring certain advantages that help people to retain information about the topics that lie within their fields of interest.

Most of the memory feats performed by retarded savants have depended upon a willingness to sustain concentrated attention for long periods of time, often extending to several hours or more. The periods of concentration have to be frequent as well as lengthy: feats that involve memorizing large bodies of information, or skills depending on memorizing, such as calendar calculating, are not gained quickly or suddenly. Lengthy exposure and practice may be required, leading to gradual improvement taking place over a period of years. In this respect the acquisition of special skills by retarded savants is not fundamentally different from skill learning in people who are more intelligent. However, in retarded individuals, unlike other people, progress may be aided by freedom from distractions in the form of competing interests and responsibilities, or personal involvements.

When people of average intelligence get lots of practice at particular memory tasks, and plenty of encouragement to do well, their feats may be just as impressive as those of savants. Henry Bennett (1983) measured the skills of cocktail-bar waitresses at remembering drink orders. Waitresses are expected to give customers their drinks quickly and efficiently: a waitress who can remember complicated orders without having to write them down can do her job better and make considerably more from tips than someone whose recall of orders is not so good. Contradicting the common belief that people's short-term memory for information in lists is unalterable, the cocktail waitresses in Bennett's study proved to be not only highly successful at remembering orders (they frequently recalled more than twenty at a time) but much better at doing so than the university students with whom they were compared in a controlled experiment. Describing a New Year's eve when the two other girls called in 'sick', and she was left on her own to take care of 150 customers, one waitress reported,

> 'By the end of the night I knew what every customer was drinking. I'd just stand by the bar, looking for hands, and give the bartender the order. Then I'd take the drinks over to the table. I really don't know how I did it.' (Bennett 1983: 165)

Another waitress told Bennett that she performed better under pressure. According to her,

> 'Regularly I have five tables so there are fifteen to twenty orders to remember. I've always done it without writing down the orders. Five years ago I had a party of 25 people. They all had separate bar and food tabs. I memorized the whole order and later wrote out all the separate checks for the food and from the bar, so I guess 50 is the most I've ever remembered at any one time.' (Bennett 1983: 164)

It is just conceivable, although highly unlikely, that cocktail-bar waitresses gravitate towards that particular job because they are good at remembering, rather than that they become good at remembering drinks as a result of the on-the-job practice they gain at doing so. But the findings of another study (Chase and Ericsson 1981) suggest otherwise. Their results show that after a great deal of practice people improve at the very simple memory task of remembering lists of digits (a task which has been thought to be sufficiently 'untrainable' to be included in standard tests of general intelligence). The authors paid a young man to spend one hour every day practising this unexciting task. The outcome, over a two-year period, was to increase his 'memory span' (the greatest number of list items that can be recalled without error) from eight items to over seventy items! To achieve this astounding improvement he made use of a number of strategies and he was especially helped by being able to draw upon a knowledge of competitive running, in which he was keenly interested. One of the techniques he used in order to help himself recall the digits was to think of sequences of digits as being running times for competitive athletic events.

Findings such as these suggest that anyone who gets a great deal of practice at recalling information in specialized areas which he is knowledgeable about may become highly skilled at remembering that particular kind of information. Just as there is nothing mysterious about acquired memory skills, there is no reason to believe that there is anything fundamentally extraordinary about the memory capacities of the majority of those individuals who gain expertise in remembering facts about a particular topic. This is equally true for retarded and non-retarded individuals.

THE IMPORTANCE OF BEING INTERESTED

If it is true that most of those mentally handicapped individuals who perform impressive feats of memorizing do not possess any exceptional basic memory capacities, they almost certainly must devote a great deal of time to their particular interests, whether or not they comprehend what they are doing as contributing to their feats of memorization. So instead of asking why some retarded savants have so much success at remembering (answer: for the same reasons as some other people do) it would be more fruitful to ask why they choose to devote so much time to their particular (often peculiar) interests. What drives these individuals to spend hour after hour concentrating on activities that most people would find boring and pointless? Why are they attracted to the odd things that interest them? What sustains their attention to such unlikely tasks?

One reason why a retarded person might choose to spend long hours on the activities that lead to substantial amounts of information being retained in memory is that the events that engage a retarded individual's attention may simply be of compelling interest to that person.

Why does a person come to be so deeply interested in a particular topic? There are many reasons, but one point worth making is that the likelihood of you or I finding something interesting enough to maintain our attention largely depends upon whether or not we have the option to turn our minds to something more interesting. This is one reason why people do not choose shops, theatres or art galleries as places for studying in: we find these environments too distracting. Any intelligent person who devotes some time to thinking about a topic as circumscribed as calendar dates will inevitably start to form connections and make associations that direct the mind to matters that are far more interesting. Perhaps such-and-such a date was a friend's birthday, and recalling this sets the person wondering what that friend is doing or remembering happenings in which he or she participated. Our minds do not linger any longer than Swann's memory rested on the taste and smell of the crumb of madeleine which, Proust tells us, brought back his flooding memories of distant Sunday mornings at Combray. All kinds of associations crowd into consciousness, even before we know it is happening.

Having a relatively sparsely furnished mind may be an advantage as far as sustaining one's attention to details is concerned. A retarded savant's sheer lack of knowledge, compared with more knowledgeable and intelligent individuals, may be one factor. For example, it may make it easier for a person to think about dates strictly as calendar information, rather than straying into the other memories that dates usually evoke. The intellectual limitations of a mentally handicapped person, perhaps combined with unusual personality characteristics, may place an individual in something like the psychological equivalent of solitary confinement. Such confinement can induce even a highly intelligent person to spend many hours counting the bricks in the wall of his cell.

MEMORY TASKS AS A MEANS TO AVOID UNPLEASANT EVENTS AND THOUGHTS

A second reason why a mentally handicapped individual may give prolonged attention to events and information that others would find uninteresting is that concentrating on inanimate objects or information can be way to avoid situations that are painful or frightening. For instance, for someone who finds it difficult to get on with other people the private and solitary nature of the mental activities that lead to details being memorized may provide a welcome relief from stressful situations.

As we have seen, a substantial proportion of mentally retarded savants are people who lack social skills and have difficulty coping with social encounters. These problems are especially acute in those individuals who are said to be autistic, but many other mentally handicapped people, perhaps the majority of those who exhibit savant skills, experience anxiety in connection with social behaviours. But memory tasks can be done in complete isolation, without any interactions with other people being necessary. Thus such tasks can provide a form of escape – a safe outlet and one that encourages a few people to direct their attention and energies in a particular (and narrow) direction. It is significant that almost all the activities at which retarded savants shine are essentially solitary ones. Moreover, mentally handicapped people rarely excel at skills that make demands on concentration if even a minimal amount of contact and co-operation with other people is also necessary. Even the limited amount of social contact that is necessary for a skill to be taught to a retarded person can form a barrier to progress: most retarded savants are essentially self-taught. The memory-dependent skills of calendar calculating and arithmetic ('lightning') calculating are both ones that substantial numbers of mentally handicapped individuals have learned with no assistance from teachers or other people. As it happens, most of the non-retarded people who have been successful lightning calculators have also taught themselves. As A.A. Brill once pointed out, arithmetic can be regarded as

> the most independent and self-sufficient of all the sciences, and given a knowledge of how to *count*, and later a few definitions, any child of average ability can go on, once his interest is aroused accidentally. Furthermore, the calculator can devote an unlimited amount of time to practice. He needs no instruments; he can carry on his research anywhere – in bed, at the table, while dressing and undressing. . . several calculators were shepherd boys with much leisure time for practice; several were sick or incapacitated for active play, and thus could devote practically all their time to practising calculation, and some, like Fuller and Buxton, were of such limited intelligence that they could scarcely comprehend anything, so that their minds were almost entirely occupied with calculations. (Brill 1940: 715)

For a small number of retarded savants, a reason for specializing in memory tasks is that concentrating one's energies in the direction of a particular narrow interest can serve to keep threatening thoughts and anxieties out of mind. By directing all one's attention to calendar dates, for example, a person may be able to block out certain unbearable ideas. In some respects the device of channelling mental activities as a means to escape thoughts that a person needs to avoid is similar to the strategy of concentrating on solitary tasks as a means of avoiding the need for social interactions. But whereas the latter may be a realistic practical response for certain mentally retarded people, there is something more decidedly pathological about having a desperate need to shut out unpleasant thoughts.

The individuals who narrowly circumscribe their interests and activities in order to guard themselves against threatening situations are often autistic or schizophrenic people, and they are by no means always mentally retarded. Certain disturbed children who have gained immense bodies of knowledge have done so about topics such as astronomy, chemistry, nuclear fission, or even finance. It was reported of one young boy,

> The one topic on which he seems interested and alive is the C——
> transportation system. Anything remotely connected with trolleys,
> buses or the subway has his immediate attention. Even a trolley
> terminal or a bus garage is a thing of fascination for him. He collects
> transfers and exchanges and will go to great lengths to secure them.
> The extent of his knowledge is amazing. He insists that his father
> used to work for the C—— Transportation Company as a trolley
> motorman. The father did take him for long trolley rides on various
> occasions but was at no time employed by the Transportation
> Company. (Robinson and Vitale 1954: 758)

Another nine-year-old boy, named Joey, was described by Bruno Bettelheim, according to whom,

> Entering the dining room, for example, he would string an
> imaginary wire from his 'energy source' – an imaginary electric
> outlet – to the table. There he 'insulated' himself with paper napkins
> and finally plugged himself in. Only then could Joey eat, for he
> firmly believed that the 'current' ran his ingestive apparatus. So
> skillful was the pantomine that one had to look twice to be sure
> there was neither wire nor outlet nor plug. (Bettelheim 1959: 223)

Human feelings and emotions were unbearable to him, and he had created machines to control his mind and body because, according to Bettelheim, 'it was painful to be human' (p. 226). Bettelheim, who considered Joey to be autistic, pointed out that many other children have a fantasy world. But unlike Joey, although they may sometimes retreat into their worlds of magic or fantasy, they can be brought back to reality. Disturbed children cannot always make the return journey.

In trying to account for Joey's difficulties, Bettelheim drew attention to a lack of warmth and affection on the part of Joey's parents. Similarly, Albert Cain has written of 'cold, intellectualized, obsessional parents turning the children into performing automata, hammering in long lists, rhymes, poems, and so on' (Cain 1969: 144), in an effort to produce child prodigies. Their children, in turn, learn that such feats provide a way of gaining parental approval, and spend more and more time on those activities, at the cost of neglecting interests and skills which are necessary for the normal development of practical and meaningful abilities.

But the vast majority of parents of those psychotic and autistic children who display special talents are quite innocent of making any effort to 'hammer in' particular feats. All the same, in some of the retarded savants who display symptoms of autism certain of the events suggested in the following account may have exerted an influence.

> More typical, in my experience, has been a pattern in which the parents, by no means obsessional, grappled in desperation for some means by which to relate to their child. Whatever had brought them to such a point, normal, smoothly interlocking parent-child cues and signals were so disordered and so poorly attuned, and most interactions so easily plunged the child into raw affects, confusion, unpredictable reactions, and unexpected panic, that both parent and child seized upon some typically innocuous facet of behaviour and interaction that offered relief. The child quickly discovered such behaviour to be one of the few sources of available praise and positive interaction. (Cain 1969: 145)

Writing of those children who combine being psychotic with possessing special skills, Cain cites a number of observations which suggest that the origin of special abilities can sometimes be related to 'desperate need states' in children. For instance, he notes that one child was first observed to be poring through calendars (an activity which eventually led to his gaining impressive calendar-calculating skills) at a time when he had just been separated from his mother.

In another child a similar interest in dates and arithmetic, which also eventually led to pronounced calculating and calendar skills, began at a time when his therapists's absence on vacation led to intense interest in the time of the therapists's return, and in his geographical location while on holiday. A third child's state of confusion and disorientation led to him making huge efforts to master skills of spatial and physical positioning. This eventually resulted in the child's acquiring the ability to retain exceptionally detailed information about the geographical locations of various places.

The skills of retarded savants share a characteristic with many of the specialized abilities of psychotic children: the abilities are essentially passive ones. They do not involve making alterations to the environment, or acting upon the world in any forceful way, or interacting to any marked extent with other people. The activities do not necessitate the child, in Cain's words, 'thrusting out' either into an external physical environment (which, for the child, is threatening and poorly understood), or towards the (equally confusing) social environment of other people. The areas of special ability are neutral and safe: they may form a barrier to shield off aspects of life which are confusing or alarming, such as those involving feelings and emotional responses that are not firmly under the individual's control.

THE REWARDS FOR MEMORY SKILLS

Paradoxically, although many retarded savants dislike activities that involve interacting with other people, savants often seem to enjoy the approval and the praise which their special skills bring them. They welcome the encouragement. A possible explanation is that the memory feats bring social rewards without incurring social costs. That is to say, having a special talent may enable someone to bask in the approving attention of other people without having to undergo the emotional wear-and-tear that comes from working with others, and which can be so alarming for handicapped individuals who lack social abilities. Especially in children, having a special talent may serve as a safe way to maintain social relationships with significant other people.

People usually repeat activities that have been rewarded in the past. the acquisition of savants' skills is sometimes helped by certain motivating events that are more especially rewarding for handicapped men and women. The effectiveness of a reward is governed by individual needs. In an experiment (Lindsley 1965) in which children's responses throughout one-hour sessions were rewarded by the opportunity to view projected still transparencies, almost all the psychotic children who served as subjects had stopped responding by the end of three sessions. This was understandable: the pictures ceased to be rewarding to most of the children, who simply got bored. But one child, unlike the others, kept on responding at a high rate of frequency throughout more than thirty of the hour-long sessions. For him, the pictures maintained their rewarding quality much longer than for the other children. How was he different? Quite simply, he, unlike the others, was deaf. Consequently, the rewarding power of visual events was especially strong and long-lasting.

One of the reasons why some retarded savants devote enormous amounts of time and attention to seemingly boring tasks may be that success at the tasks and the encouragement they receive may be particularly rewarding for them. Rewards which would not satisfy most people may have a very powerful effect on a mentally handicapped individual. For example, with a skill like calendar calculating, although for most people getting a right answer would not be a sufficient reward for the tiresome work involved, for a few mentally retarded individuals getting something correct may constitute a very powerful reward. Also, having a special skill may give an inarticulate child or adult a way of expressing individuality and getting attention and recognition as a unique, 'special' person. Such a skill may help a person to maintain relationships with others and provide one way to exert some control over important aspects of the individual's environment. Like everyone else, mentally handicapped people enjoy the feelings of achievement and self-respect that they gain from succeeding at something. Yet there are harsh limits on the varieties of success they can achieve. It makes good sense for such individuals to specialize by carefully directing any talents they possess, thereby maximizing the likelihood of becoming competent at the particular activity which they pursue.

CAN SPECIAL MEMORY FEARS CAUSE OR CONTRIBUTE TO MENTAL RETARDATION?

For various reasons, retarded individuals often become narrower, or more 'channelled' or 'canalized' in their interests than normal people. A possibility that we have not yet considered is that the special abilities of a retarded savant may actually have a role in *causing* certain aspects of a child's mental retardation or autism. It is conceivable, for example, that the developing ego of a young child may be threatened by certain reactions of other people to the extent that the child is pressed towards repetitive or stereotyped patterns of behaviour. This could result in certain specialized skills being acquired at the expense of other needed developments which, in normal children, are integrated with key aspects of the individual's intellect and personality. Some investigators have observed behaviour in certain parents which could have had such an effect. In other circumstances the acquisition of normal abilities may be inhibited by specialized talents which function, as do certain pathological symptoms and bizarre patterns of behaviour, to give a person some control over aspects of a life which seems to be out of control (Nurcombe and Parker 1964). For instance, a schizophrenic patient is described by David Forrest (1969) as having tried to structure his environment and avoid the feelings of loss of control that threatened him by gathering sixteen clocks around himself and spending virtually all his time typing.

ARE CERTAIN FEATS EASIER FOR MENTALLY RETARDED INDIVIDUALS?

Some investigators have suggested that deficits in mental functioning can actually make it easier, rather than more difficult, for an individual to do certain tasks. In some mentally handicapped individuals it is possible that their very deficiences have had the effect of removing barriers that would prevent a normal child from acquiring certain special skills. For example, the absence of symbolic abilities may make it easier for a person to concentrate on surface features such as the physical attributes of events that (for normal people) have a symbolic function. When a normal child sees the same events, the fact that the meanings or deeper attributes of objects are attended serves to distract attention from the surface aspects.

For similar reasons, as Ogden Lindsley (1965) has noted, young children whose symbolic behaviours are very limited but who do have the ability to make perceptual discriminations, are often more successful than individuals with normal symbolic skills at those learning tasks which involve making such discriminations. Therefore, Lindsley argues, behavioural deficits may be an advantage in a few specific environments. In children with restricted language abilities, 'their limited symbolic repertoire apparently prevents them from entertaining many irrelevant and time-consuming hypotheses as they go about solving a learning problem' (Lindsley 1965: 228).

Individuals who lack symbolic and abstracting skills will have a decided advantage in those situations in which the abstracting capacities that most people utilize spontaneously serve to distract attention from crucial attributes. For instance, an idiot savant who does calendar calculations may be well suited to concentrating on calendar dates precisely because he is not hampered by the kinds of ideas and associations that crowd in when most people look at a calendar. Again, a savant artist's concentration on shapes and the physical dimensions of objects may be assisted by the decreased likelihood, compared with other people, of attention shifting away from the physical dimensions of seen objects and towards their meaning.

For the idiot savant, avoidance of distractions caused by the representational and symbolic qualities of objects in the world comes about with no effort, as a result of an absence of normal cognitive processing. In normal people a degree of relief from distracting thoughts can sometimes be achieved by deliberately shutting off competing information. Some blind people seem to have special auditory skills, such as the ability to listen to echoes bounced off nearby objects. Lindsley (1965) reports that the well known early jazz and street musician, 'Blind Lemon', attributed his own musical skills to his blindness. Another street musician, 'Moon Dog', actually blinded himself in order to escape the distraction of sights as he went about his musical activities in the streets of New York.

Research findings support the view that intellectual deficits can sometimes improve rather than retard performance at learning tasks. In one study, for example, intelligent college students were compared with mentally retarded people (mean IQ = 58) at a task in which they were shown successive pairs of Japanese symbols: they had to decide which item was the 'correct' one. In fact the correct item was always the one in the position (right or left) that was different to that of the correct item in the previous pair. The authors reasoned that mentally retarded subjects would do well at this task because their responses would be governed by arbitrary preferences for particular items or by response decisions that took no account of the nature of the particular items. The more intelligent subjects were expected to base their responses on hypotheses about the attributes of the various Japanese symbols. Such an approach, although normally sound, did not lead to success in this particular task. Thus the mentally handicapped subjects, simply because their responses were less likely to be governed by inappropriate hypotheses, were expected to be more successful. The findings confirmed this expectation. The retarded subjects correctly alternated their responses on seventy-five per cent of occasions, significantly above chance level. The performance of the college students was considerably worse.

Although it is unusual for mentally retarded participants to do better at learning and memory tasks than people whose intelligence is normal, it is not difficult to find situations in which comparisions between normal people and retarded individuals reveal no differences in favour of the more able learners. For example, W.K. Estes (1970) concludes that studies comparing individuals of widely varying levels of intelligence at simple learning tasks based on classical conditioning reveal no systematic relationships at all between performance and ability. Similarly, the usual superiority of adults compared with young children at learning and memory tasks tends to disappear when opportunities for learners to make use of effective strategies are eliminated (Belmont 1978) or when the nature of the tasks prevents older subjects from taking advantage of their greater knowledge (Ceci and Howe 1978). In short, there are numerous occasions on which mentally retarded learners can be expected to perform just as well as able people. When this fact is coupled with the observations that certain tasks are more interesting to retarded than to normal people, that limited success may be more rewarding to retarded individuals, and that in some circumstances retarded learners may be less liable to be distracted by misleading items of information, it becomes hardly surprising that under certain conditions the achievements of retarded people do actually surpass those of highly intelligent learners.

HYPERLEXIA

As we have seen, there are circumstnaces in which being mentally retarded can give a person distinct advantages. For example, certain memory achievements are facilitated by an absence of the distracting thoughts that impede a person's concentration on some kinds of detailed information. Is it possible that qualities associated with mental retardation can positively benefit performance at certain tasks? And are there any skills which retarded savants can achieve but which are quite impossible for people of average or even superior intelligence?

Surprising as it may seem, in one or two instances this does appear to be the case. One example is that of the uncanny drawing skills produced by a mentally retarded child, Nadia. Lorna Selfe (1977) has reported that from the age of three years this little girl produced large numbers of drawings that are far more accurate and realistic than anything within the capabilities of even the most intelligent children of twice her age. In her case (which will be discussed in Chapter 6) the literal accuracy of the drawings was linked to and dependent upon the fact that her understanding of the meanings of seen objects was gravely deficient.

Further instances of skills that are closely linked to mental deficits are observed in a small number of children who have been labelled 'hyperlexic' – a term that refers to their unusual reading abilities. These children can 'read' with considerable fluency, but without genuine comprehension. This skill appears to be based on an ability to memorize letter–sound correspondences despite having little awareness of what words actually mean. Some cases have been reported of mentally retarded children who have been able to decode textual passages at the age of only two years. Typically, such children are autistic, and they do not use language spontaneously to communicate with others. Some hyperlexic children also possess other skills, sometimes ones encountered in idiots savants, such as calendar calculating. Their reading often appears to have an involuntary quality. For example, on entering a room a hyperlexic child may

> seize any reading material and begin to read aloud in an ritualistic fashion. The reading is so compulsive that it is hard to stop, it proceeds by the child's disregarding semantic information, indifferent to whether the materials are drawn from a primer, a technical journal, or a collection of nonsense. (Gardner 1984: 85)

A hyperlexic child may be capable of reading words that are upside down. In the case of one four-year-old,

> The mother first discovered that he could sound out words when he read 'SNOINO' on a can which had 'ONIONS' printed on it and which was standing upside down. At the age of four years ten months he read a third-grade reading paragraph fluently. He obviously enjoyed this skill and he wanted to read any material in sight, but his understanding of spoken speech continued to be poor. . . . (Huttenlocher and Huttenlocher 1973: 1,108)

Another child, whose spontaneous speech was restricted to poorly pronounced single words, read numerous words by the age of two, and by three he regularly read newspapers, dictionaries, telephone books and everything else he came across. Yet another individual, who at the age of eight had no intelligible speech and was unable to feed himself, is described as having roamed the office where he was being examined, 'reading from diplomas and certificates, even those in Latin' (Mehegan and Dreifuss 1972: 1,108).

Although there has been considerable speculation on the matter, precisely how it is that hyperlexic young children are able to succeed at 'reading' difficult written materials is something of a mystery. Almost certainly, however, very extensive memory for particular letter– and word–sound combinations is involved, and in all probability this odd skill depends upon normal understanding of the meanings of words being absent (Aram and Healy 1988).

ARE RETARDED SAVANTS INCAPABLE OF ABSTRACT THINKING?

In a number of the attempts made to understand retarded individuals with savant capabilities emphasis has been placed on the view that a deficient ability to reason abstractly is an important contributing factor. The case history of Richard is one example. In fact, the combination of a normal or near-normal ability to remember with restricted powers of abstraction is encountered in a large proportion of retarded savants. Is it possible that the absence of abstract thought provides a key to understanding retarded savants' limitations, and perhaps a clue to their special skills as well?

Defining abstract thought is not easy. Broadly speaking, the level of abstraction in a person's thinking can be regarded as an indication of the extent to which deep meanings are involved, and the degree to which the content of thought is removed from the superficial qualities, or surface structure, of the information or events being processed. People who lack abstracting abilities can think only in a highly concrete manner. Up to a point it is possible to measure the degree of abstractness of a person's thought, or at least of the *products* of a person's cognition. But using the concept of abstraction, not simply in order to indicate the product of thinking but also to describe the *mechanisms* of cognition, introduces problems. For instance, it is not easy to specify exactly what is different between more and less abstract thought, except in terms of the consequences.

Mentally retarded people are undoubtedly handicapped at abstract reasoning. In their report of the investigation of Richard, described in Chapter 2, Scheerer and his co-authors (1945) noted that an 'impairment of abstract attitude' can affect behaviour in a wide range of circumstances. In Richard, for example, intellectual functioning was handicapped by his failure to appreciate the symbolic or conceptual meanings that are expressed by language. Thus he did not grasp the properties of objects, such as size, form or category membership. Moreover, achievements like discerning similarities, differences, opposites or common denominators, or perceiving metaphors and logical analogies, were all impossible for him. His use of language was highly concrete, bound to particular situations, and largely based upon particular conditioned verbal responses that he made mechanically whenever certain environmental cues were present. Richard's defective abstract reasoning was central to many of the limitations in various aspects of his life, such as his social behaviour, his reactions to new and disturbing situations, his performance at tasks requiring planning or organization, and his failure to generalize or apply the arithmetic skills he possessed.

There is little doubt that deficiencies in the ability to think abstractly have a central place in the limitations we find in retarded savants and other mentally handicapped people. However, the explanatory value of this observation is limited, since our understanding of the cognitive mechanisms underlying mental abstraction and of the causes of individual differences in abstracting abilities is relatively meagre. To complicate matters, there are variations *within* individuals in the extent to which the ability for reasoning abstractly is deficient.

It is tempting to think of a person as having a general ability to think abstractly, and to infer that the lack of such an ability is a cause of failure at various intellectual tasks. But such a view is almost certainly wrong, and it is probably more accurate to regard the level of abstraction in a person's reasoning as being tied to, and dependent upon, the factors operating in particular situations. People are often able to think abstractly in certain aspects of their lives but not others. Rather than thinking of abstract reasoning as a general skill or trait which permeates many abilities, it is more realistic to perceive the degree of abstractness of a person's thought concerning a particular topic as being closely tied to the individual's knowledge of that topic.

In short, it is quite wrong to think of abstract thinking as a general-purpose skill that permeates, or can be applied to, different mental abilities. The case of Harriet provides a convincing demonstration.

In connection with music she often showed feelings and emotions, and she acted spontaneously and flexibly, in a manner which we would regard as indicating a high degree of intelligence, and making heavy demands upon an ability to think in abstract terms. Outside music, however, her thought and behaviour were tightly restricted to the concrete and the particular. Such a contrast in levels of thought within a single person shows that whilst it can often be valuable to discuss the abstractness of someone's thinking when *describing* a person, introducing the concept of abstraction in order to *explain* mental strengths and weaknesses is logically indefensible.

The evidence of this chapter points to the conclusion that the causes of retarded savants' memory feats lie in the special circumstances of these people, and not in fundamentally special skills or mechanisms of memory. The unusual lives of some individuals tilt them towards activities that eventually lead to extraordinary feats of remembering: certain of the limitations associated with mental retardation work to remove obstacles to memory achievements that are thrown up in the everyday lives of most people. But the demonstration that an individual can be simultaneously gifted and retarded continues to be a source of bafflement: it is a contradiction of our beliefs about the structure of human abilities. This issue is addressed in Chapter 4.

Chapter Four

THE INDEPENDENCE OF HUMAN SKILLS

In Chapter 3 I started to explain how it is possible for certain mentally retarded individuals to succeed at impressive feats of remembering. This chapter continues and broadens the attempt to understand retarded savants and their achievements. Most of the published reports have included an effort of some kind to explain the particular feats that are described in them but few of the many questions that arise have been properly answered.

FORMS OF EXPLANATION

Attempts to explain puzzling phenomena are not always fruitful, even when they are manifestly sensible and correct. Although most authors who have written about retarded savants have tried to provide some insight into the phenomena they describe, the explanations advanced have too often been ones that do little to increase our real understanding. For example, in a number of the earlier accounts it was suggested that injury or damage to the brain was a contributing factor. Unfortunately, most of these reports have little or nothing to say about the precise causes of the damage, or about the detailed form it has taken. They are equally silent about the exact way in which the injury to the brain might have affected the individual. On reflection, simply stating that a person's thinking is defective because something is physically wrong with his brain is not particularly illuminating when no details are provided. Moreover, even if it is true that damage to the brain was a cause of a person's disabilities, knowing this alone does little to help us answer the more important question of how that person came to have the particular combination of deficits and talents that is characteristic of mentally handicapped savants. Similar criticisms apply to the suggested explanations that accompany a number of published accounts of idiots savants. These have introduced a variety of possible causes, including epilepsy, syphilis, encephalitis, organic disease, aberrations in hemispheric localization, and several other physiological dysfunctions. Again, the manner in which these might have actually influenced the person is never specified in any detail at all.

Some authors have argued for explanations that are based on psychodynamic interpretations of the events in a person's life. Often these are insightful and thought-provoking, but they always suffer from the vital handicap of being quite impossible to verify or disprove. If the psychodynamic accounts are to be believed, particular events that take place in unconscious mental life are invariably behind an individuals's difficulties. For example, it has been suggested that giving prolonged attention to the task of memorizing (or 'taking in') large numbers of facts may represent a person's unconscious desire to undo or compensate for the loss of narcissistic play, as a result of the enforced removal of faeces in childhood.

Psychodynamic interpretations like the one above may serve to clarify our thinking about handicapped people with particular talents. They draw attention to the extent to which behaviour can be driven by needs of which the individual is completely unaware. All the same, with the majority of psychodynamic explanations, it is impossible to ignore the fact that it is virtually impossible to see how they could ever be conclusively verified, and this is a major limitation. The trouble with such accounts is that they invoke an array of hypothesized events that are said to have taken place but which can never be observed, even indirectly. It is certainly true to say that we are not conscious of much of the mental processing that is going on in our heads whenever we think, but to accept a psychodynamic explanation is to acknowledge far more than this. It involves agreeing with a large number of untestable assertions about the unconscious products of our (unconscious) mental processing activities. Without ruling out the possibility that the achievements of idiots savants may remain incomprehensible unless we accept psychodynamic explanations based on the actions of unconscious forces, we would do well to bear in mind that when we start to investigate something it is a good scientific strategy to begin by concentrating on those phenomena that can be observed and measured without too much difficulty.

Most of the many different questions that will need to be answered if we are to have a complete understanding of retarded savants fall into one or other of two kinds. First, there are queries, such as the ones about remembering which we started to answer in Chapter 3, about how it might be possible for a mentally handicapped person, one whose ability to deal with any kind of mental task appears to be highly restricted, to succeed at the highly impressive feats which retarded savants are seen to perform. How can such individuals achieve these feats, in the face of what seem to be overwhelming obstacles? Or, to put things into a different perspective by reversing the question, how can somebody who is an expert at certain difficult achievements be so inadequate at other skills that seem to be much easier?

Second, how are the feats actually done? There are many questions about the ways in which retarded savants are able to achieve and perform their skills. For instance, how are the different abilities learned? What sequence of mental operations is carried out in undertaking a feat of, say, mental arithmetic or calendar calculating? When a retarded savant performs a skill, is more or less reliance placed on memorization than when the same skill is done by a person of greater intelligence? What do mentally retarded calendar calculators actually *do* in order to produce correct answers to questions about dates and days of the week?

Questions of this second kind receive a good deal of attention in Chapters 5 and 6. The present chapter concentrates on exploring the contrasts in retarded savants' abilities to do different things. The aim is to discover how it is possible for a single person's different skills to be so divergent, fragmentary, and apparently independent of one another. How can the same individual be simultaneously exceedingly talented (at music, for example) and incapable of meeting even the most modest demands of day-to-day living.

AUTONOMOUS SKILLS AND ABILITIES

Since it is the contrasts and divergences that are most baffling, we might do worse than start by asking why it is that we should find such divergences so puzzling. Why do we assume that this is something that needs to be explained? Why shouldn't a person's different skills be autonomous and fragmentary, and why are we so surprised to find that they are? What are our reasons for anticipating otherwise? Why do we not expect to encounter isolated mental feats?

I suggest that the main reason lies in our having an implicit view of the nature, organization and control of human abilities which is inaccurate and misleading. That is to say, we share a flawed conceptualization of the manner in which different abilities are related to each other, and the reason for our being so puzzled by individuals who are simultaneously talented and retarded is that they contradict it. In sum, the patterns of skills observed in retarded savants appear paradoxical only because of the way in which we think about mental abilities. In trying to understand these people, who so clearly contradict any conclusions arising from such thinking, we are forced to make explicit certain views that are normally implicit and unexamined. At the same time we are made aware that certain of our broader beliefs about the nature of human abilities rest on assumptions that are, at best, highly questionable.

Common sense, strongly backed by a long tradition of psychometric research into mental abilities, tells us that each of us is intelligent to a certain degree, and that, broadly speaking, how well or how badly we do at tasks that are intellectually demanding depends on how intelligent we are. Someone who is highly intelligent, or 'bright', or 'clever' can reliably be expected to perform better at any of a variety of mental challenges than an unintelligent, or 'dull', or 'dim' individual. If asked to explain why a person has been unusually successful at any of a range of problems that demand mental abilities similar to the ones that are measured in an IQ test, we are content to answer by saying that the reason is because he or she is intelligent. We would be equally willing to accept that another person's failure at the same problems may have been caused by a lack of intelligence.

This widely accepted view appears to receive support from the fact that in the vast majority of people levels of abilities at different mental achievements are undoubtedly related to each other, even though profiles showing any individual's actual performance at different mental skills are somewhat irregular. It is accepted that someone may be better at (say) science than languages, but, it is assumed, only within definite limits can achievements in particular areas be independent of a person's general level of ability. The level or amount of a person's intelligence is seen as an important determinant of success: in the absence of enough intelligence it is quite impossible for an individual to gain achievements that depend upon intellectual skills. Thus intelligence is regarded as indispensable for doing well at certain tasks. It can be stretched and redirected in various ways, but only up to a point, and there is no compensating for a total lack of it.

The truth of the matter is that such a view is quite wrong. It reflects a faulty understanding of the nature of human ability. Contrary to the implications of that viewpoint, in which particular mental abilities are seen as at least partly governed by intelligence, there are strong empirical grounds for believing that it is quite possible for a person of any intelligence level to possess skills that are unrelated to general ability. But before introducing the evidence for this assertion, I think it necessary to anticipate a possible objection. The objection is that the common-sense view by which achievements are seen as being constrained by intelligence, even if widely held by unenlightened people, is not one that is accepted nowadays by professional psychologists who use ability tests or by researchers who measure intellectual abilities, and is therfore a straw man.

It is true that those who have undertaken research into human intelligence have drawn attention to a variety of separate ability factors, profiles of abilities, mental dimensions, and structures, and that although the centrality of a general intelligence factor (or 'g', which was defined by Charles Spearman as mental energy or force) is frequently emphasized, the point is occasionally made that the existence of such a factor does not necessarily imply that it has a strictly causal influence. Nevertheless, within the powerful psychometric tradition of research into individual differences in human attributes it is widely accepted that general ability underlies all cognitive performance, even when specific abilities are also involved. It is also believed that the organization of abilities is likely to be hierarchical, with general mental ability having a controlling influence over particular achievements.

The score obtained on an intelligence test is no more than a broad indication of someone's degree of success at dealing with a range of problems that require intellectual skills. But it is all too easy to forget this and to slip into the error of thinking of high intelligence as being the real cause of someone's success. Even those psychologists who admit that the existence of a 'g' factor need not imply cause-and-effect frequently talk of intelligence level as a reason for doing well or badly at a mental task. But in reality, the conceptual status of intelligence as it is actually measured is broadly on a par with that of a concept such as 'productivity'. Introducing measured intelligence in order to explain someone's expertise at a task is logically equivalent to saying that the reason why a factory makes lots of cars is because it is a highly productive factory. In both cases the so-called explanations are 'correct' but largely empty of meaning, except as restatements.

In recent years researchers studying individual differences in cognitive abilities from information-processing and computational perspectives have been critical of the traditional psychometric approach to intelligence (see, for example, Sternberg and Salter, 1982). And there exists a large body of neuropsychological evidence which is not easily reconciled with an approach in which general intelligence is seen as exerting a governing role. But amongst most psychologists, especially those who make use of intelligence tests for practical purposes, for example in clinical, educational or vocational practice, as well as in the field of mental handicap, the psychometric assumptions underlying construction of ability tests are widely shared and rarely challenged. One obstacle to clear thinking about the nature and causes of people's abilities is that the idea that general intelligence is a cause of a person's level of performance at particular tasks is so firmly entrenched that simply mentioning the word intelligence at all, when an individual's abilities are being discussed, is taken to imply the existence of intelligence as some kind of controlling process that limits that person's achievements.

In fact, there are strong reasons for arguing that, despite all appearances, it is not actually the case that intelligence constrains a person's achievements at particular mental skills. On the contrary, in people of all levels of mental ability it is quite possible for isolated mental skills to exist, ones that are largely independent of the individual's measured intelligence. It follows that the achievements of mentally handicapped savants, however unusual they may be, ought not to astonish us. In the light of this alternative viewpoint they are simply extreme instances of the permissible autonomy and independent functioning of any person's distinct mental skills.

If it is true that many mental skills can operate separately, rather than being centrally controlled, we would expect to find that large differences between a single individual's levels of mental functioning at different achievements can be observed in highly intelligent people as well as in mentally handicapped ones. Do such differences really exist? Answering this empirical question presents no insuperable difficulties, and some of the evidence will be examined shortly.

In practice the discrepancies may not appear to be quite so prominent when the superior skills are not set off against the background of an unusually low profile of other abilities. And there is another reason for large differences between the levels of a single individual's mental skills being especially noticeable when they occur in a mentally handicapped individual. This is that the interests towards which talents are directed are often ones that seem especially odd or bizarre to ordinary people, or are ones (for example, calendar calculating) on which we find it strange that someone would choose to spend large amounts of time. And the fact that retarded savants tend to be individuals who 'specialize' in particular feats to an extent which may be rare among people of normal ability may provide one more reason for our attention being more likely to be drawn to savants than to ordinary people whose mental skills are equivalently uneven.

The idea that a person's different abilities may be largely independent of each other may appear to fly in the face of the facts of everyday life. After all, there are large positive within-individual correlations between mental abilities. The everyday commonplace that people who are good at one skill that demands mental abilities tend to be good at other mental skills as well is supported by a vast array of correlational evidence obtained from research into mental measurement. So, too, is the claim that a 'bright' person can reliably be predicted to perform better than 'dull' one at a wide range of tasks. If intelligence tests did not produce useful predictions they would have been discarded long ago. And the pattern of correlations that emerges when performance levels at different specific skills are correlated with each other is consistent with the view that mental skills are hierarchically arranged, with general ability at the apex of the hierarchy.

However, it is important to bear in mind that the presence of correlations between a person's skills does no more than indicate a state of affairs whereby, in most people, different mental skills tend to coexist with each other. There is no justification for making any inferences about the underlying causes that bring about this situation. The individual measures and the correlations between them are nothing more than end products of whatever processes give rise to them. The fact that a correlation is seen to exist provides no reason to justify making any statement about why there is a relationship between the measures, or about how the relationship came about. And the finding that there are positive correlations between measures of a person's success at different skills gives no grounds at all for concluding that the measured skills must be centrally controlled by that person's general ability or intelligence, or even that they must be centrally controlled at all, let alone for inferring that any mechanisms involved are hierarchically organized.

But if different human abilities were genuinely distinct and independent, wouldn't we expect that there would be no relationship at all between them? As we have seen, substantial correlations are common. How do they arise? If I wish to argue that the observed relationships between different mental abilities cannot be taken as evidence that separate abilities are centrally governed, or constrained by some kind of general ability, I have an obligation to say how else they might be explained.

As it happens, it is not at all difficult to explain the existence of such correlations. There is no need at all to conclude that they inevitably point to the existence of an underlying general mental ability. People tend to leap to such a conclusion, perhaps because it is a plausible one, or perhaps because it may appear to be the simplest way to account for the relationships. In fact, there are two straightfoward reasons which, between them, quite adequately account for the greater part of, and possibly all, the observed correlations. The first reason for different performance measures at mental tasks being correlated is quite simply that many tasks require more than one mental skill. Moreover, many skills have shared elements. Hence the correlations between measures of performance at two tasks may reflect the fact that to some extent each is drawing on the same skills or on skills that have elements in common.

The second reason underlying the correlations in a person's degree of success at different mental tasks is that even when the latter do not involve mental skills or elements that are common to each, performance at all the tasks (or some of them) may be affected by certain enduring qualities of the individual. Personal attributes that are likely to affect the likelihood of someone being successful at each of a variety of tasks include ones that determine the degree to which a person is skilled at attending, anxious to succeed, interested in certain kinds of problems, knowledgeable, patient, competitive, assertive, persevering and self-confident. In consequence there will be a correlation in measures of performance at those different tasks to which any of the various attributes can make a contribution. And when the correlations that arise from personal qualities which affect performance at a number of different tasks are combined with the effects of the previously mentioned influence (different tasks having shared, common elements or depending on identical skills) the joint outcome may be very substantial. Consequently, it is quite unnecessary to introduce the idea of a governing general mental ability, or intelligence, in order to account for the fact that within-individual abilities are seen to be related. Such a mechanism is redundant: the correlations it exists to explain are already accounted for.

Although the fact that different tasks share elements in common and depend upon similar personal qualities will often lead to different measures of mental performance being related to one another, this will not always or inevitably happen. In this respect the effects of these influences are quite unlike the ones that are supposed to occur as a result of a general mental ability. If the latter really was an important influence, it would permeate *all* tasks that involve mental skills. In contrast, there is no such inevitability about the other causes of performance correlations. For instance, a person who is usually attentive might do relatively well at tasks that interest her but not at all well at those which bore her. Conversely, someone who is normally impulsive and readily distracted might perform rather poorly on the majority of tests but nevertheless be successful at one or two pursuits which happen to catch his interest and engage his concentration. A person's level of performance at two tasks that share common elements will amost certainly be correlated, but there is no reason to expect similar correlations in performance at those tasks that do not have shared elements, except on those occasions where personal traits that are brought to each of a number of tasks provide an alternative reason for the degree of success.

The main point is that whilst the two reasons we have mentioned will often lead to there being relationships in the level of performance at two or more tasks, there is nothing automatic or inevitable about this. That is because the correlation is not produced by any basic process or mechanism that is shared by all the tasks. As a consequence, there will be many occasions on which measures of ability are quite unrelated. Relatively independent and autonomous mental abilities are not ruled out, whatever the level of a person's measured general intelligence.

To summarize the argument in the current chapter up to this point, it is suggested that the divergences and discrepancies in mental functioning within individuals that are so noticeable in idiots savants may in fact be found in people at all levels of intelligence. The contrast is an extreme manifestation of mental arrangements that are a universal feature of the human condition. It is not just an anomaly reflecting some curiosity of nature caused by defective cognition in mentally handicapped people. The fact that intra-individual correlations in mental-test performance are often observed is not due to different tasks being centrally controlled by a general ability factor (which would lead to all of a person's mental abilities being correlated with one another, whereas they manifestly are not), but to their either containing shared elements or being affected by shared personal traits.

In practice it is unlikely that large discrepancies in achievement levels will be so frequent in people having normal ability levels as in the mentally handicapped, or that particular feats and skills will be quite so isolated or fragmentary. One reason for this is that, for a number of reasons, intelligent people are better at transferring, generalizing and applying their existing skills to new circumstances and different contexts. Whenever it is conceivable that a new task may utilize an already learned skill, it is more likely that the existing skill will actually occur if the individual is an intellectually able person than if a mentally handicapped person is involved. As a result, the sharing of identical skills in different tasks will be more common in more capable individuals. But all the same, large discrepancies can occur and (as we shall see) do occur in people of all kinds.

EVIDENCE OF INTRA-INDIVIDUAL DIFFERENCES IN MENTAL ABILITIES

Up to this point, although it has been argued that the kinds of differences I have been discussing *can* exist in people of all levels of ability, no hard facts have been supplied to prove that they actually *do* (except in the case of mentally retarded savants). What evidence is there on this matter?

There is no substantial body of psychological literature that directly addresses the issue of intra-individual differences in normal cognition, because researchers have not thought it necessary or useful to look for such differences. When psychologists have investigated patterns of ability within individuals they have almost looked for similarities rather than differences. They have done so for sound practical reasons, mostly related to the endeavour of constructing mental tests and measuring instruments to help professionals working in disciplines such as education or vocational assessment and selection to make useful predictions about people's capabilities. From the perspective of anyone who is mainly concerned with down-to-earth issues of this kind, the similarities in scores are clearly more interesting than the differences. Consequently, the relationships and correlations between mental scores have received much more attention than the differences between those scores. The fact that irregularities and discrepancies are noticeable whenever one examines profiles of human abilities has not gone entirely unnoticed, but since it has not been easy to see how to make use of this knowledge (whereas the practical benefits of knowing about positive correlations are obvious enough) the differences have never been given much attention.

Some of the evidence of large divergences in people's mental skills is straightforwardly anecdotal. Stories of individuals whose brilliance at chess, mathematics, science, or whatever, contrasts with glaring deficiencies in other spheres are common enough. Of course, such anecdotes are hardly a reliable source of information but it is interesting to note from autobiographical sources that some of the most powerful thinkers have believed themselves to have been less than adequate in certain areas. Take, for example, the brilliant mathematician, Norbert Wiener, who first drew attention to himself as a child prodigy, began his university education at the age of eleven, and gained a doctoral degree at eighteen. Despite his early brilliance it was not until he was seven that he discovered that Santa Claus does not exist. As he later reported in his own words,

> at that time I was already reading books of more than slight difficulty, and it seemed to my parents that a child who was doing this should have no difficulty in discarding what to them was obviously a sentimental fiction. What they did not realize was the fragmentariness of the child's world. (Wiener 1953: 81)

Charles Darwin included in his autobiography a self-appraisal of his own mental skills. One is struck by the contrasts, even after making allowances for the inevitable subjectivity. He is not falsely modest about his own strengths, a fact which lends credence to what he says about areas of weakness. Darwin wrote,

> I have no great quickness of apprehension or wit. . . . My power to follow a long and purely abstract train of thought is very limited; I should, moreover, never have succeeded with metaphysics or mathematics. . . . So poor in one sense is my memory, that I have never been able to remember for more than a few days a single date or a line or poetry. (Darwin 1958: 140)

Darwin's cousin, Francis Galton, another major Victorian thinker and the founder of eugenics, gives an interesting insight into the unevenness of mental abilities in a precocious eight-year-old. Recalling his school, he noted,

> In that room was a wardrobe full of schoolbooks ready for issue. It is some measure of the naivety of my mind that I wondered for long how the books could have been kept so fresh and clean for nearly two thousand years, thinking that the copies of Caesar's commentaries were contemporary with Caesar himself. (Forrest 1974: 8)

The fragmentariness of children's skills that is remarked upon in these anecdotal accounts has also been observed in investigations that are more systematic. For instance, a study of eight-year-olds who were exceptionally talented chess players revealed that they were perfectly normal in other spheres (Feldman, 1982). And the transcripts of interviews in which highly gifted young adults talk about their childhoods, supplemented by interviews with their parents, are full of testimonies to the extreme ordinariness of the individuals, outside their particular area of special talent (Bloom 1985).

Cross-cultural research is a further rich source of evidence that people who, to Western eyes, appear to be intellectually very limited in many respects, can at the same time be highly expert at cognitive skills that are dauntingly complex. For instance, simple mental problems caused severe difficulties to the Micronesian navigators investigated by Tom Gladwin (1970), despite the fact that these remarkable people not only possess very considerable amounts of knowledge about navigation but are expert at making subtle inferences and sophisticated judgements, and at doing impressive calculations, in order to find their way around the perplexing seas they inhabit.

Another way of observing the independence and autonomy of different mental skills is by examining the extent to which abilities are correlated. This may seem to be a paradoxical suggestion, since I have previously drawn attention to the fact that correlational evidence is customarily used in order to demonstrate the reverse, i.e. that different abilities are indeed related. It is undeniably true that, in some people, some test scores are related to one another. Yet it is equally true that, so long as the individual scores genuinely reflect performance at particular distinct skills (rather than being agglomerations of scores obtained from sampling performance at a variety of different skills), correlations tend to be very low or non-existent. Such findings have not received the attention they deserve.

The above point is illustrated by examining measures of relationships between intelligence and learning. Intelligence is widely thought to be related to ability to learn (and some investigators have actually defined intelligence as being learning ability). But contrary to expectations, whenever systematic studies have been undertaken to assess the actual relationships between measures of intelligence and performance at particular learning tasks, the correlations have turned out to be either extremely low or non-existent. In other words, there is no substantial relationship between them at all. In fact, profoundly retarded individuals have been found to perform just as well as highly educated adults at certain forms of learning, such as classical conditioning (Estes 1970). In a variety of learning tasks, systematic differences in expertise between people of varying intellectual ability have been found to be remarkable mainly by their absence.

So measured intelligence and 'learning ability' are by no means the same thing, after all. Moreover, on the many occasions when investigators have calculated the correlations between performance at different tasks of learning, these also have been found to be either zero or very low. The probably reason is that in actuality there is no such thing as a unitary learning ability that is common to different kinds of learning. It appears that learning skills are highly specific. That is why performance at one kind of learning task provides little or no indication of the likelihood of success at a task that requires a different form of learning.

Similarly, when people's performance levels at a number of different memory tests are compared, the magnitude of the inter-task correlations is again extremely low. For example, in a study in which five-year-olds were each given eleven distinct tests of memory and the experimenters then computed the correlations between each child's different test scores (Stevenson *et al.* 1975), the correlations averaged only $+0.14$. (Even when statistically significant, correlations of this magnitude are virtually useless for making predictions about individuals.) So, just as the hard evidence shows that it is inappropriate to speak of a general learning ability that permeates most or all different kinds of learning, it is equally wrong to imagine that there exists a general ability to remember that influences performance at all memory tasks. Rather than thinking of people as having 'a good memory' or a bad one, it would be more realistic to appreciate that how well something is remembered will depend upon a number of highly specific factors, ones that are tied to the particular task and also to various contextual features, such as the particular domain of knowledge involved. As a rule, as was noted in Chapter 3, people are good at recalling information about matters that interest them and things they are knowledgeable about. It is only when two learning or memory tasks are very similar to one another that substantial inter-task correlations are found.

More information showing that a person's different abilities are less closely related to one another than we might expect has been provided by studies investigating the relationships between measures of intelligence and measures of success at various life skills. Again, contrary to what would be expected were it true that different mental abilities are closely connected and under some kind of central control, it emerges that a number of important measures of success in the real world are uncorrelated with measured intelligence. The correlation between IQ scores in childhood and measures of effectiveness at the everyday tasks of post-school life is only around $+0.20$ (McClelland 1973), and in moderately retarded people who have moved away from institutions their adjustment to daily living has been found to be quite unrelated to intelligence test measures (Zigler and Seitz 1982). Furthermore, the success of men with some degree of mental handicap at adjusting to military life in the US army was also found to be unrelated to IQ.

A large amount of further evidence concerning the independence of different mental skills and the extent to which fragmented abilities can exist in isolation comes from an entirely different source — research into the effects of brain damage. Studies investigating the outcome of such damage show that the effects of brain lesions on human skills can be remarkably specific. Obviously, a brain-damaged person is highly abnormal: the functioning of a damaged brain is never the same as the working of an intact one (Mehler *et al*. 1984). Even so, if it can be shown that a particular skill or ability is capable of functioning when certain similar skills are inoperative, to a degree which would be inconceivable if the different skills were totally interdependent, we can deduce that centralization is less than total.

To cite a few instances from a large body of empirical data, studies of language deficits (aphasias) show that damage in the part of the left hemisphere, known as Broca's area, can lead to a person talking in a manner that depends on short phrases involving simple propositions and substantives, with few function words and inflections. Despite their speech problems, people with lesions in Broca's area may be fairly good at understanding language. Damage to a different part of the left hemisphere, known as Wernicke's area, leads to a very different form of aphasia. People who have suffered lesions in this part of the brain may retain the ability to speak fluently and in complex grammatical sentences, but the content and meaning is liable to be unclear. Their ability to comprehend language is also poor. Lesions in a third part of the brain, the angular gyrus, produce yet another distinct pattern of deficits. Here, damage leads to an inability to locate the particular words and names a speaker needs, so that speech is filled with terms like 'kind of', 'things', and 'stuff'. Circumlocutions like these ones reflect a person's inability to retrieve from memory the particular language items that are required. A brain-injured person may suffer total loss of memory for language and verbal materials and yet retain the capacity to remember large amounts of complex information in the form of patterns of physical behaviour and motor sequences. This can lead to a person carrying out a sequence of complicated activities that depends upon them having been remembered from previous occasions, while at the same time denying that the sequence has ever been encountered before.

The effects of those injuries that do lead to impairments in motor activities (apraxias) can also be very specific. An apraxis individual may be capable of understanding a request to undertake certain actions and also physically capable of doing so, but unable to carry out the appropriate activities in the correct sequence. Depending on the precise location of the damage, a person may fail to transfer an activity from one hand to the other, or be incapable of putting his clothes on, or lack the capacity to execute particular sub-tasks that are necessary for running smoothly through a sequence of ordered actions. Often, of course, damage to the brain will lead to a combination of disabilities. Even so, the particular combination may be highly distinctive. With the Gerstmann syndrome, for instance, following damage to the angular gyrus, left-right orientation, drawing, calculating and certain finger skills may be lost whilst other intellectual abilities stay intact.

Some aphasic people who have lost the ability to use language can nevertheless manage to do calculations and simple arithmetic; others keep their language but lose their calculating skills. Individuals in the former group may be able to manage their financial affairs. They can pay for items in shops and work out the change, and even play games in which calculating is necessary, in spite of having overwhelming language disorders. A particular area in the region of the left parietal lobes and the adjoining temporal and occipital associative areas appears to have a special importance for mental capacities underlying logic and mathematics.

The condition known as pure alexia provides an especially striking illustration of the distinctiveness of the mechanisms that underlie calculating abilities on the one hand, and language skills on the other. Sufferers from this condition can understand symbols and read numbers so long as these items are encountered in the context of numbers and arithmetic. But the same people cannot read word items that surround the numbers. One such person could identify DIX as being the Roman number for 509 but he could not read the same letter sequence as a language syllable (Gardner 1984). The fact that he could 'read' the syllable as a Roman numeral demonstrates that he had no difficulty in perceiving the materials. It was the particular decoding requirement of written language that caused difficulties for him. The effects of other brain lesions can be equally specific. A person can experience selective losses in particular numerical capacities. The ability to produce mathematical symbols and decode them appears to be regulated largely by the left hemisphere of the brain, whilst comprehending the concepts and relationships encountered in arithmetic depends to a greater extent on mechanisms located in the right hemisphere. As a result, losses are correspondingly selective: the capacity to understand the meaning of a sign that refers to a numerical operation may disappear whilst other numerical abilities are largely unaffected. Alternatively, a person may retain the capacity to understand signs but cease to comprehend the actual operations.

Certain musical abilities appear to be regulated by parts of the brain that are distinct from those involved in either language or calculating skills. Taking in pitch details, for example, depends on mechanisms that are separate from the ones that process non-musical sounds such as those encountered in language. The separation between these functions has been investigated in some ingenious experiments (Deutsch 1975). For example, in one study individuals were told to remember a set of auditory tones which they listened to. Then they heard some more, similar, sounds. These tend to 'interfere' with recall of the original items. It was found that when the second set of sounds took the form of verbal materials, such as lists of numbers, the interference with subjects' memory for the original tones was very much less than when the intervening sounds were other auditory tones. The reductions in recall of the original tones following the interpolated second sets of sounds were, respectively, as little as two per cent and as much as forty per cent.

There are definite limitations to what can legitimately be inferred from research findings demonstrating the effects of localized brain damage on human capacities. Locating an area of the brain that is associated with a particular deficit does not explain how the affected behaviour is controlled, although it may provide useful clues. Also, the finding that damage to a certain part of the brain affects a mental skill does not prove either that the area in question is uniquely responsible for that skill or that the area does not also contribute to other capacities. All the same, whenever it is discovered that brain damage in particular regions affects different mental capacities in a highly selective manner, we are justified in inferring that there is a degree of separation and autonomy in the mental processing operations that underly the different capacities.

The evidence concerning the effects of various kinds of brain damage is large and growing. For example, there is a substantial body of findings concerning the relationships between brain dysfunctions and specific reading disabilities. And lesions may affect various aspects of a person's personality, temperament, mood, self-consciousness and self-awareness, without having much influence upon problem-solving abilities and other cognitive functions, and vice versa. Howard Gardner (1975) contrasts the case of an injured Russian soldier who, despite suffering appalling damage to the brain involving destruction of many kinds of symbolic abilities, managed nevertheless to keep intact his sense of identity, with the experiences of other brain-injured patients who have suffered lesions in the frontal lobes. In these patients, who may have had only minor problems with intellectual skills, there is extensive damage to the personality. Depending on the particular lesions that have occurred, such people may be hyperactive, irritable, apathetic, listless, depressed, indifferent or euphoric, and no longer recognizable by their friends and relations as being the 'same person' as before.

In retaining a firm sense of his own identity, it could be said that the Russian soldier, unlike the patients with frontal lobe damage, maintained a higher degree of conscious awareness of who he was. Conscious self-awareness seems to be essential for one's continuing identity as the 'same person'. It was noted in Chapter 3 that some surprisingly high-level intellectual functions can be undertaken without the person concerned being at all aware of them, but the absence of consciousness can have devastating and bizarre effects. Individuals suffering from 'cortical blindness', in whom the visual cortex (situated at the back of the brain) has been destroyed, have the experience of being completely blind in the affected areas of their visual field. If they are asked whether they can see a light, or an object, their reports will clearly indicate blindness. However, if an object is placed in the affected area, and the patient persuaded to 'guess' where it might be, certain of these individuals will not only 'guess' the exact position with considerable accuracy but will also 'guess' the objects's shape correctly or accurately 'guess' whether lines are horizontal, vertical or diagonal (Weiskrantz *et al.* 1974). In this rare conditions it seems that the function of seeing is somehow maintained without the person having any corresponding conscious experience of vision. Equally remarkable, a patient who, so far as conscious vision was concerned was effectively blind for light of certain wavelengths and therefore perceived red objects as being black or grey, was nevertheless able to construct stereoscopic images when a red pattern was presented to one eye and a green pattern to the other. Since stereo vision depends upon light of both the appropriate frequences being detected, it is clear that this individual's brain did in fact receive and transmit certain visual signals which his conscious mind failed to 'see'.

To people who are fortunate enough to be both intelligent and sane, experience is all of a piece. By and large, everything hangs together. There seems to be a controlling self, a continuing and dependable identity. Yet although this experience is no illusion, it is a description of the outcome of the detailed operations of a healthy brain rather than a description of how those actual operations work. We experience our own mental lives as being integrated and coherent, but only because the separate functions of the brain work together in a coordinated fashion.

It is realistic to speak of the brain functioning as a whole that is far more than the sum of the parts; yet the separate parts are nevertheless vital, and can vary independently in their strengths and weaknesses. We experience only 'the whole': it takes the evidence provided by unusual people in whom mental integration is incomplete owing to retardation, brain damage or some other kind of mental 'disturbance' to make us appreciate how the smooth functioning of a person's total mental system depends on the parts, or sub-systems, that underlie it.

CO-ORDINATING MENTAL ACTIVITIES

The case against the view that mental skills are largely governed, hierarchically or otherwise, by an unitary general ability is a strong one and raises an important question. It is this: If separate abilities are not centrally controlled, how are they co-ordinated? Where every single mental mechanism to operate entirely on its own, without reference to other cognitive functions, the result would be total chaos. The human brain is not just a collection of isolated functions. Many of its activities must be tightly co-ordinated if it is to work effectively. The discovery that skills can operate with a considerable degree of independence and autonomy should not obscure the fact that there are numerous connections between the different brain systems. However distinct the parts are, they have to work together, in harmony if not in unison. The task of trying to understand how mental co-ordination is achieved is far too daunting to be attempted here, but a few thoughts on the matter are in order.

It is useful to make a distinction between co-ordination, which is clearly present in the working of the brain's parts, and centralized control. The latter may appear to be a possible way of achieving co-ordination, but it is not the only way. As the neurologist Norman Geschwind remarked,

> What we have learned is that the brain really is a kind of federation and, furthermore, a loose federation; it is not perfectly connected. The extent of the disunity varies from person to person. In any case, there does not appear to be a central prime mover overseeing all behaviour. (Geschwind 1983: 127)

But our conscious minds seem to tell us otherwise. I experience a single 'me', who seems to be in charge of things, and my brain's activity seems to be all of a piece. Yet my conscious perception of my own mental activities as being unified under the command of a governing 'me' is illusory. The unity of conscious experience is possibly a by-product of the largely verbal activity of trying to interpret and report the contents of our mental lives to our conscious selves. In his extended essay, *The Modularity of Mind*, Fodor (1983) provides detailed arguments for the view that 'many fundamentally different kinds of psychological mechanisms must be postulated in order to explain the facts of mental life'. He shows that each mental module (or group of mechanisms), although connected to other modules, also needs to have firm boundaries. The claim by Geschwind that the brain is a rather loose federation of imperfectly connected parts is echoed in a suggestion that the mind is analogous to a sociological entity made up from numerous elements:

> The mind is not a psychological entity but a sociological entity, being composed of many submental systems. . . . The uniqueness of man, in this regard, is his ability to verbalize and, in so doing, create a personal sense of conscious reality out of the multiple systems present. (Gazzaniga and Le Doux 1978)

The brains of many different species, including sub-mammalian ones, are capable of highly complex activities, but these are usually more specialized than in human beings. In the human brain, partly because of the great number of connections between the different sub-systems, the parts can operate together with a high degree of co-ordination, and this makes it possible for particular processes and functions to be directed to a number of separate purposes.

Intelligent humans are able to access any of a variety of different mental operations, enabling co-ordinated use to be made of them. This capacity is by no means universal in living organisms. Of course, a large number of sub-mammalian species display very impressive skills, involving lengthy and complex sequences of closely regulated events. These are very specialized, however, and accessible only in very specific conditions. In fact, circumstances in which 'lower' organisms have access to their mental sub-systems are rigidly circumscribed: there is no possibility at all of a mental mechanism that has evolved in order to provide one particular function being utilized for a different task. The mental superiority of the higher species does not depend on their being greater complexity or sophistication of the particular brain systems underlying single skills. Rather, as Paul Rozin (1976) has emphasized, the advantages lie in the extent to which the brain's different systems, or subprograms, are accessible in a range of alternative circumstances, and are consequently capable of performing multiple functions. If Rozin is correct, the greater powers of human brains compared with sub-mammalian ones owes more to differences in the accessibility of different functions than to differences in the capacity or complexity of the functions.

Rozin notes that human abilities use a large number of sub-programs, which he terms 'adaptive specializations'. Adaptive specializations are capacities to do particular things. They are found in a wide range of species and can be extremely complex, even in species that would not be regarded as being intelligent. A well known instance of a successful adaptive specialization is the system by which honey bees are able to exploit food sources, as described by von Frisch. Despite having brains which are no larger than the head of a pin, bees can store and communicate detailed information about the distance and direction of sources of food. For this achievement to be possible it is necessary to have mechanisms for making allowance for the varying position of the sun. It is necessary for the bee's brain to have considerable knowledge of astronomy and also an internal clock that is needed for making appropriate use of that knowledge.

As a consequence of the lack of easy accessibility to different subsystems of the brain, lower species suffer from the limitation that their adaptive specializations (such as the food-seeking system of bees) are generally unavailable to the other brain mechanisms possessed by the same organism. In Rozins's words, 'At the time of their origin, these specializations are tightly wired into the functional system they were designed to serve and are thus inaccessible to other programs or systems in the brain' (Rozin 1976: 246). The different systems each operate in relative isolation: they cannot be combined with, or utilized by, any other specialized capacities which the same organism may possess. In higher species, on the other hand, with their more highly organized and interconnected brains, particular systems tend to be more widely accessible. Their greater availability makes it possible for an animal to utilize for a varity of new purposes brain systems that were originally developed for a particular, often quite different, function. The more widely accessible are the specific systems of the brain, the more likely it becomes that the brain can operate flexibly, by altering and extending its activities adaptively in ways that utilize devices for organizing, combining, co-ordinating and duplicating the various different subprograms.

Certain kinds of neural dysfunctioning in the human brain are caused by destruction of the connections between different brain systems rather than by damage to the systems as such. Systems that normally function together in a co-ordinated manner can remain isolated, with results paralleling in some respects the kinds of specialization of isolated functions that occurs naturally in lower species. It is just conceivable that the manifestation in retarded savants of single abilities which are on the one hand impressively complex but on the other hand apparently unconnected to other capacities, contrasting with the greater degree of connectedness and co-ordination between different functions that is typically observed in normal people, could stem from a similar separation of brain systems, resulting in a lack of accessibility between the different specialized parts. Yet there is no positive evidence at all that that is the case. In autistic individuals, however, there is a greater likelihood that the state of affairs indicated in the above account may exist.

Undoubtedly, functions that are normally co-ordinated do sometimes become disconnected from each other. This happens with some kinds of brain damage. For example, it has been known for patients to experience a sudden loss of the ability to read, accompanied by blindness in the right visual field but with no loss of perception in the left visual field. The underlying cause of this unusual combination of symptoms is a brain lesion which has severed essential connections between different brain systems. Another kind of disconnection (caused by damage to the complex system of neural connecting tissues known as the corpus callosum) was the cause of the bizarre behaviour of a woman examined by Kurt Goldstein early in the present century. He observed that she would start to choke herself with her left hand, whilst the right hand would simultaneously try to pull the left hand away from the neck. She repeatedly insisted that her left hand was beyond her control. It appeared that brain damage had caused a separation between functions which we ordinarily assume can only operate together and in a co-ordinated fashion.

It is not being claimed that in retarded savants there is a complete physical severance between different functions of the brain, such as can occur following brain damage. Nevertheless, it is quite possible that there is a degree of disassociation between elements that usually function together and in a co-ordinated manner. Some kind of separation between normally interdependent functions may well be a contributing factor to the manifestation in retarded savants of isolated particular abilities which operate at high levels of efficiency whilst the flexible and adaptive behaviour which enables normal people to have independent and effective lives is unhappily absent.

As we have seen, although the divergence between levels of ability in different areas of functioning is particularly remarkable in retarded savants, as is the related high degree of separation between functions which in normal adults appear to work together, neither of these phenomena is at all rare in everyday life. They are particularly common amongst groups of individuals who are either immature or mentally retarded. In young children, for instance, many skills when first acquired are very fragile and inflexible. Their availability at that time is likely to be restricted to the particular circumstances in which they were initially learned. Young children's new skills do not readily transfer to new tasks and unfamiliar situations.

The capacity to apply newly acquired skills to a variety of different circumstances is a hallmark of a person who is experienced and mature: it has to be learned, and does not emerge automatically. Whereas it may be obvious to a mature and intelligent person that a particular ability is widely applicable to many different situations, for the immature or mentally handicapped person who has only recently gained that skill it may be very tightly welded to the sphere of activity in which it was initially acquired. A child of normal intelligence may fairly rapidly learn to extend the range of circumstances in which it is possible to gain access to a particular skill and make use of it, so that the skill begins to take on a 'multi-purpose' nature. But in a mentally handicapped person the ability to use the same skill in alternative contexts can remain extremely restricted throughout life.

Being able to apply mental skills adaptively, to connect them together when it is appropriate to do so, and to modify them in order to meet the demands of new tasks, are all fundamental to the flexible behaviour of capable people. The absence of such flexibility is possibly more important as a cause of the contrasting achievements of mentally superior and mentally handicapped people than is the presence or absence of any particular skills. As I have suggested, large discrepancies between levels of mental performance in different areas, which are so strikingly apparent in retarded savants, are most accurately regarded not as phenomena which are unique to mentally retarded individuals but as particularly forcible demonstrations of one important reason for the differing capabilities of people in general.

ARE THERE MULTIPLE INTELLIGENCES?

Since the idea that each individual possesses a unitary intelligence that limits success at intellectual skills fails to stand up against the contradictory evidence, it may be best to restrict scientific use of the concept of intelligence to purely descriptive purposes. An alternative proposal, which Howard Gardner puts forward in *Frames of Mind* (1984), is to replace the notion of a single intelligence by a model of human ability according to which each person has a number of separate and largely autonomous intelligences. The attraction of this proposal lies in its appearing to reconcile the conceptual framework of the intelligence-testing approach to mental abilities with the empirical finding that different abilities are not in fact nearly so interdependent as they would be if that approach was basically correct. With Gardner's alternative model, a child who is good at music but not at mathematics would be said to have high musical intelligence and low mathematical intelligence.

Obviously, for this new approach to provide a coherent alternative there would need to be a limit to the number of abilities that can be designated as forming separate intelligences: one cannot simply carve the landscape of mental activities into a plethora of arbitrarily-bounded principalities. There must be some rules or principles to determine when an ability or group of abilities can be said to form an intelligence. In particular, if the model is to have credibility it must be possible to ensure that skills resting in different intelligence are genuinely independent, and that performances at different skills that are within the field of a single intelligence are indeed related.

In attempting to provide a model of multiple intelligences which achieves these aims, Gardner argues that it is reasonable to think of a particular area of ability as forming a distinct intelligence only when there is supporting evidence from a number of different sources. In general, he feels that a case can be made for the existence of a particular form of intelligence when the area of competence is one that may become highly developed in particular cultures and when it is possible to define the abilities that underly it. In order to decide whether any 'candidate' sphere of competence should be included among the intelligences, Gardner lists eight down-to-earth criteria. These are: first, that the 'intelligence' can be isolated by brain damage (the extent to which an ability can be destroyed or spared in isolation of other abilities being a clear indication of autonomy); second, that evidence from exceptional individuals exists to show that it can be selectively present or absent; third, that there is some identifiable core operation or set of operations; fourth, that there is a distinctive developmental history in which different levels of expertise can be identified; fifth, that an evolutionary history exists (Gardner thinks that the roots of current human intelligences go back millions of years); sixth, that there is support from experimental psychology, for example, from experiments assessing the autonomy of skills by measuring transfer and interference effects; seventh, that psychometric findings give support (which will often take the form of the correlations that may provide the sole criteria for decisions in psychometric approaches to intelligence); and eighth, that the underlying computational capacity can be embodied in a system of symbols that have meaning within a culture (which would not be true, for example, with the mechanisms that are responsible for controlling the digestive system).

Any area of ability which exhibited all eight of the above criteria would be classified as a separate intelligence, and any candidate which exhibited no more than one or two of them would not. Gardner would not exclude a candidate just because it did not qualify on all eight criteria: he is vague about the fate of a candidate intelligence which met, say, four or five of the eight criteria. Gardner lists six candidate intelligences which he considers to meet a sufficient number of the above criteria. These are linguistic intelligence, musical intelligence, logico-mathematical intelligence, spatial intelligence, bodily-kinesthetic intelligence, and a group of abilities which he calls the personal intelligences.

The extent to which the multiple-intelligence approach will catch on remains to be seen. Acceptance of it would have important practical implications, especially for education. There are unresolved problems: one is that each single intelligence reproduces certain of the features that cause difficulties in the unitary intelligence approach; another is that despite the existence of seemingly objective criteria for deciding on the acceptability of candidates for inclusion in the list of intelligences, a degree of vagueness remains. For instance, there is no clear statement concerning the number of criteria that have to be met, and with some of the criteria (the third, for instance) it is not always clear how one would know if they were met. All the same, the approach will prove valuable even if it only succeeds in provoking careful thought about the structure and organization of intellectual abilities. It forces us to be more aware of the relative independence of many human abilities, to think about the implications, and to appreciate the limitations of current approaches to intelligence.

INSIGHT AND CONSCIOUSNESS

People who are made aware of the difficulty of explaining how retarded savants can achieve the feats they demonstrate sometimes make the perfectly sensible suggestion that one might ask the individual concerned to say precisely what he or she is doing. To what extent are people actually aware of their own mental processes, and conscious of the inner workings of their brains?

Some investigators have spent hours talking to retarded savants to try to elicit from them the means by which their achievements were made possible. On the whole the answers have not proved particularly illuminating. Fairly typical is the response of the young calendar calculator who Julia Smith and I questioned (see pp. 113–28). 'Use me brain' was his stock reply to queries about the means by which he arrived at correct answers to difficult calendar questions. Sometimes he altered his response, but only to 'Use me head'.

Any frustration we may feel with the barrenness of retarded savants' self-reports can be tempered by the knowledge that even the most intelligent individuals are surprisingly unsuccessful when they try to describe the mental processes that make it possible to do intellectual tasks. Most people are inclined to believe that the conscious self has a reasonably full understanding of the ways by which our brains undertake tasks that involve mental skills such as reasoning, comprehending, calculating and problem-solving. In fact, experimental psychologists who have tried to assess the actual accuracy of self-reports as a guide to the actual sequences of operations that people's brains perform as they carry out mental tasks, have repeatedly been surprised to discover just how inadequate are people's introspections concerning even the most basic activities of their mental lives. We may like to think that the conscious self is at the centre of our mental operations, firmly in command, and fully informed about what is going on. The reality is somewhat different. Consciousness appears to have only a limited and surprisingly ineffective controlling function.

One author (Jaynes 1976) has made the provocative claim that only within the past three or four thousand years have humans actually become fully conscious of what they are doing. He argues that until comparatively recently people behaved, talked, produced written reports, and performed many of the activities that we engage in ourselves without being conscious of what they were doing. This bold assertion need not be taken too seriously: the evidence for it is less than convincing, though undoubtedly fascinating. But the fact that a serious scholar can even make such a claim, however outrageous is seems, should alert us to the fact that common-sense notions about the role of conscious thought in our own lives ought not to be taken for granted. Much can be achieved in the absence of any awareness. And even if there is no truth at all in the assertion that people in ancient societies were not conscious, it is still possible that individuals in different cultures are not all self-aware in exactly the same way.

Moreover, psychological research has clearly established that the conscious self is ill-informed about many of the operations of the brain, including those ones that are responsible for the most complex forms of intellectual thought and decision-making. The role of consciousness in relation to the brain's activities has been linked by the philosopher Daniel Dennett to that of a poorly informed official who is supposed to take charge of a company's public relations. He is expected to communicate knowledge about his organization to the outside world but he is not sufficiently accurately informed about the activities and decisions made by that organization to do a particularly good job of communicating, let alone to have much control over whatever the organization does (Dennett 1983). Empirical investigations by psychologists have confirmed that our access to the activity of our own minds is very restricted indeed. In consequence, even among the most intelligent and 'self-aware' individuals, the reality is that,

> And so the notion, which was overpoweringly obvious to somebody like John Locke or Descartes, that the mind is transparent to itself, that each one of us is the ultimate authority on everything that's going on in our minds, that we are incorrigible, infallible observers of our own mental life, has been completely overthrown. (Dennett 1983: 80)

Such a negative assessment of the executive power and the knowledgeability of the conscious self may strike some readers as contradicting experience and common sense. Nevertheless, the evidence leaves us no reason for doubting that, despite any contrary intuitions we may have, we often totally fail to 'know what we are doing', so far at the thinking processes of our own brains are concerned. So, asking people – however bright or dull they are, talented, gifted or otherwise – how their minds achieve their goals is unlikely to produce much useful information. Beyond a point, nobody has the slightest idea what his own brain is up to.

Chapter Five

CALENDAR CALCULATING

Most of the skills of retarded savants are ones which are also done by ordinary people. In this respect calendar calculating is very different. In perhaps a third of the published case histories the person is reported as having the ability to solve problems involving calendar dates, although people of normal ability hardly ever learn this particular skill. Nor do we find calendar calculating in normal children. The activities that ordinary children and adults get involved in include some remarkable ways of passing the time but calculating calendar dates is not among them.

The fact that calendar calculating is often reported in case histories of idiots savants may give a misleading impression of the true rate of occurrence: simply because the skill is so unusual it is more likely to be noticed and talked about than commoner feats that demand mental skills of equivalent difficulty. Nevertheless, the number of cases is substantial. It is not at all obvious either how certain retarded savants are able to do calendar calculations or why so many of them turn their energies in that particular direction. We shall try to answer these questions in the present chapter.

The usual way to test someone's ability to perform calendar calculations is to give questions asking for the day of the week on which a given date falls. For example, the question might be, 'On what day of the week is 8 May 1984?' The span of time over which a particular retarded savant can answer questions like this one may be as small as a couple of years or as large as several centuries. Some retarded savants can also solve other kinds of calendar problems, for example, 'What is the date of the second Tuesday in May 1984?', or 'In what years between 1970 and 1980 does 8 May fall on a Tuesday?'

In many of the reported cases, only the first kind of question has been asked, and it is not at all clear whether or not the individual would have been capable of solving the alternative types of problem. In order to make progress towards discovery how a particular retarded savant does calendar calculations we have to ask various different kinds of questions about calendar dates. We can then narrow down the range of possible methods that might have been followed, since certain methods will enable a person to answer some types of questions but not others. For convenience, we shall use the term 'calendar calculating' simply as a descriptive label for the feat of being able to answer questions about calendar dates. No implication that a person is necessarily 'calculating' in a narrow sense of the word is intended.

Whatever the particular method being followed, solving calendar problems that involve dates spanning many years calls for skills and knowledge that are not needed for answering questions about dates over a span of just a year or two. The latter might be achieved by sheer memory alone, without any calculations as such being required. With longer spans it is probably necessary to be able to count forwards and backwards from particular remembered dates, which may function as 'base' days. Counting, perhaps aided by simple addition, would allow a person who knows, for instance, that 6 May 1984 fell on a Sunday to deduce that 8 May must have been a Tuesday. Other kinds of knowledge that might help a person to do calendar calculations, especially ones involving years in the distant past or future, include knowing that each arrangement of the days in a month falls into one of seven basic patterns, knowing the timing of leap years, and how they influence calendars, knowing about the exclusions to leap year rules at the ends of centuries, and knowing when calendars repeat themselves and how the arrangements of dates within a month repeat themselves.

There is a temptation to leap to the conclusion that because an ordinary person's chances of being able to do a certain task would be increased by his having a particular item of knowledge, a retarded savant who can perform the same task must also possess the knowledge in question. That is not necessarily the case. As we shall see, the methods by which a retarded person achieves success at a calendar task can be very different from the ones which an intelligent individual would follow, if faced with an identical task. It is especially easy to underestimate what savants can achieve by sheer memorization alone. Most of us hate having to memorize large amounts of information but a retarded savant may be quite happy to follow an approach that makes very considerable demands upon memorizing, even though, as an intelligent person would quickly perceive, there is an 'easier' alternative method which places much less stress upon memory.

SOME CASE HISTORIES

Descriptions of calendar calculating in retarded savants began to appear well before the present century. Most of the more recent reports include some attempt to explain how the subject is able to perform the feat, but the earlier accounts are usually somewhat sketchy. For example the 1920 report by Hiram Byrd about the man from Oxford, Mississippi, mentioned in Chapter 1, simply records that if he was told the month, day and year for a date between 1901 and 1924, he would supply the correct day of the week, with no failures and no hesitations. He also gave the correct answer if asked about the day of the week of, say, the second Tuesday or the fourth Friday of any particular month and year. Byrd reported that university students used to test the man with old calendars, and that he provided 'a never ending source of entertainment for them' (Byrd, 1920: 202). Byrd did raise the question of how to account for his subject's ability to name dates, and mentioned that the man kept a notebook in which names and train numbers were recorded. But the means by which calendar answers were produced remained a complete mystery. Similarly, in a case originally reported in 1909 (Jones 1926), a twenty-year-old man was said to be able to give the correct day of the week for any given date between the years 1000 and 2000. Again, however, the investigator was unable to discover how the feat was achieved.

There is an intriguing description of calendar calculating skills in a young man who had no speech at all (Roberts 1945). The man was physically handicapped: he suffered from spasticity and could not walk. Because of his physical deficits it was difficult to judge how mentally retarded he actually was. He responded by nodding or shaking his head if he was asked calendar questions, such as 'Is it Monday?', 'Is it Tuesday?', and so on. When tested in this way he could correctly specify days of the week for any dates between 1915 and 1943. He made errors only occasionally.

Whenever he was asked a question about a date, the young man gazed at the ceiling before he responded. This suggested to the investigator that some kind of visual imagery was being used. The results of a number of small-scale experiments designed to test that suggestion proved interesting, if not entirely conclusive. For example, Roberts found that the man did well at a picture memory task, but he was not at all successful at recalling a visual display of digits. Later, he was shown a calendar for the year 1945, in which each date was coloured red, green or black, the different colours being allocated at random. He studied the calendar for over two hours. Two days later he was asked to indicate the day of the week for a number of dates in the calendar. He answered all the questions correctly. For each date he was also questioned about its colour. On the first occasion he was incorrect at first, but when the investigator advised him to 'look at it again' he looked up at the ceiling, gave the right answer, and then correctly answered all but one of eleven further questions at the first attempt, always gazing at the ceiling before responding.

These observations provide some support for the view that what the young man was doing included making use of some kind of visual imagery. As it happens, the suggestion that visual images may contribute to calendar calculating is one that has been put forward by several of the investigators who have made serious attempts to account for calendar calculating skills in idiots savants.

However, another case history demonstrates that even if it is true that some feats of calendar calculating by retarded savants involve the use of visual imagery, others definitely do not. The report describes calendar calculating skills in a sixteen-year-old girl who was totally blind, and had been so from infancy (Rubin and Monaghan 1965). When she was ten years of age the girl's parents discovered that she could name the day of the week on which certain dates had occurred. At this time her twin sister had a similar ability. The twin had some sight and a higher level of general intelligence than her blind sister, but as the years went by the sighted twin's calendar skills did not improve. However, the blind twin was encouraged by her teacher to develop her ability to do calendar calculations. Her success at them, together with the attention she was given whenever she performed the skill, became important for her: she would tell visitors about herself by shouting out, 'I'm a calendar girl'.

The extent of this blind girl's achievements was not comaprable to the most exceptional accomplishments in sighted idiots savants, either in the length of the span of years over which she could answer questions or in the proportion of her responses that were correct. All the same, her skill was impressive. Once, one of the investigators gave her a list of 40 dates, five being taken from each of the years between

1958 and 1965. She told him the correct day for 27 out of the 40 dates, and on half of the occasions when she made an error she was just one day out. A possible explanation for these mistakes is that she had failed to take into account the fact that 1964 was a leap year. Except for the two years 1964 and 1965 she gave the right answer for over 80 per cent of the dates. When she was tested again (on the following day) with the same dates the number of correct answers rose to over 90 per cent. It is clear that this girl was able to perform difficult calendar calculations despite being totally blind.

The evidence that calendar calculating can be done by someone who has been blind since infancy appears to rule out the suggestion that visual imagery is indispensable for the performance of such a skill by a mentally handicapped person, unless one makes the implausible assumption that visual imagery is available to individuals who have been blind since birth. But in the absence of contradictory evidence, it is still conceivable that the most impressive calendar feats of all, ones which involve spans of hundreds or even thousands of years, can only be achieved if the individual is able to draw upon visual imagery.

The present case of a blind calendar calculator also raises broader questions about the extent to which the different individuals who perform the feat all use identical or similar methods. At first sight it may seem likely that since a substantial number of idiots savants share the ability to perform this task, which hardly any non-retarded people can do, the methods of different savants must all be similar if not identical. But as it happens, the findings of some of the more thorough investigations are not at all consistent with such a view. There are major differences between retarded savants in the ways they perform feats of calendar calculating.

In most of the reported cases, once an individual gains calendar calculating skills he or she holds on to them for at least a substantial number of years, if not permanently. One exception is a Finnish woman who, when tested at the age of seventeen, could do calendar calculations over a fifty-year range (Palo and Kivalo 1977). Like most retarded savants she enjoyed performing her skill: she gained obvious pleasure from demonstrating it to visitors who came to the hospital in Helsinki where she was examined. But after two years the ability gradually disappeared. When she was tested in her mid-twenties she refused to cooperate in calendar calculation tests, and she seemed to have lost the skill. In her case the disappearance of calendar calculating ability was one aspect of a general deterioration in mental functioning, probably connected with a collagen metabolism defect that was reflected in decreasing activities and declining intelligence test scores.

There are more than enough case histories to establish the fact that calendar calculators exist in reasonably substantial numbers among mentally handicapped people in a number of continents. But it is not easy to discover precisely what are the mental skills underlying a person's ability to do calendar feats, or to find out how the skills were acquired in the first place. In order to make real progress towards understanding how people gain calendar skills and discover how the various feats are achieved, it has been necessary to undertake investigations that are more thorough and extensive than the ones mentioned above.

That is not to deny that some of the briefer investigations of calendar calculations have thrown up some interesting ideas. They have. For example, David Viscott mentions that in the case of Harriet (Chapter 2) her calendar calculating skills depended on the fact that she knew several hundred days by rote. She made use of these days as 'anchors' when asked about other dates. (In fact, if she was given a date, as well as specifying correctly the day of the week it fell on she would often recall the weather report and mention one or two items from that day's news, and, what is more, tell the interviewer what she ate for dinner on the same day!) And Richard's (Chapter 2) responses to calendar questions (Scheerer *et al.* 1945) often included what appeared to have been tantalizing clues to the methods by which he solved the problems. For instance, when asked 'Which day is 10 June 1938?' he quickly mumbled '20, 31, 30, 31, 30, 30, 31, 31, 28, 31, 30, 31, 10', before giving the correct answer 'Friday'. Clearly, knowing the number of days in each month played some part in his approach. Richard also seemed to have made use of a knowledge of how the days are patterned *within* a month, as he showed by remarking that '10, 3, 17, 24 always gives Friday.'

But the most illuminating studies have been ones which have gone well beyond observing and describing the most easily noticed abilities of calendar calculators. These more substantial investigations have made systematic use of carefully formulated questions and tests that were designed to assess the person's capabilities. A major aim has been to discover how savants have been able to co-ordinate a number of relatively simple sub-skills in order to be successful at calendar calculating, which is undoubtedly a complicated task.

SOME CALENDAR RULES

Before we describe some of the more ambitious investigations, consider
the first difficulty that faces a scientist intending to examine calendar
calculating in mentally retarded individuals. How does one start? How
do we begin to investigate a phenomenon which appears so alien to
most people? In the absence of other clues, a possible starting point
is to imagine how a person of normal intelligence might do calendar
calculations. Although it is unlikely that a mentally handicapped person
would follow the same methods, as I said before, such a strategy has
two advantages. First, it generates ideas, albeit improbable ones, about
possible procedures that retarded savants might conceivably follow.
Second, it gives us valuable information about ways in which calendar
calculating *can* be done. This may increase our understanding of the
requirements of the skill and the kinds of knowledge that a person might
be able to utilize in order to perform it.

Published methods for doing calendar calculations are fairly readily
available. Descriptions of such methods are to be found in a few diaries,
in certain handbooks, and in occasional works of reference and general
knowledge. In their procedural details the alternative methods differ
considerably, but they all make use of the fact that the arrangements
of days in a month and months in a year are organized systematically,
following a few simple rules. Since every month must start on one of
seven days, each arrangement of the days in a month must fall into
one of only seven basic forms, the only added complication being the
fact that not all months have the same number of days. It follows,
incidentally, that if I know the exact configuration of days in each of
the seven types of calendar month (perhaps aided by a visual image
of each) and if I can discover which of the seven a particular month
falls into, it will be easy to calculate the day of the week for any date
in that month.

The relationships between the configuration of a particular calendar
month and the ones preceding and succeeding it are not arbitrary,
although the varying numbers of days in different months complicates
matters. However, because each month (except February) always has
the same number of days, the ordering of the different types of calendar
months shows a rule-governed, repeatable pattern. And calendars
repeat themselves every 28 years. Thus 1 August 1988 is a Monday,
and in 2016, 2044 and 2072 1 August will also fall on a Monday.

Leap years appear at regular four-yearly intervals, except at the beginning year of three new centuries out of four, and it is not difficult to take them into account in a system for performing calendar calculations. The reason for having leap years is that the 'true' length of each year, defined by the time taken for the Earth to circumvent the sun, is about a quarter of a day over 365 days. Inserting an extra day every four years roughly compensates for the fact that the length of the year is not an exact number of days. But the astronomical year is less than *exactly* a quarter of a day longer than 365 days, so it is necessary to introduce occasional additional adjustments. This is achieved by making a few of the years that would otherwise be leap years into 365-day years. The procedure that has been adopted is to make each year at the beginning of a century a non-leap year, unless it is divisible by 400 (as are, for example, 1600, 2000). In these cases the leap year status is retained.

DEVICES FOR CALENDAR DATE CALCULATIONS

Because calendars obey fairly straightforward rules, it is not too difficult to devise a formula or algorithm, or a series of tables incorporating the rules, that will enable the user to find the right day of the week for any date that can be specified. There are a number of alternative methods: they all achieve the same and result, but in different ways. Some require the user to consult a series of tables, constructed according to the constraints outlined above. The tables direct the user through a number of stages, leading eventually to the correct day of the week. Other symptoms guide the user into following rules that generate the correct answer. This can be achieved, for example, by the following set of instructions:

1. Take the last two digits of the year
2. Divide by 4 and ignore remainder
3. Add the date within the month
4. Add the code number from the following list corresponding to the month: Jan = 1, Feb = 4*, March = 4, Apr = 0, May = 2, June = 5, July = 0, Aug = 3, September = 5, Oct = 1, Nov = 4, Dec = 6. (* denotes subtract 1 for leap years)
5. Add steps 1 to 4
6. Divide by 7. Remainder is the day of the week (1 = Sun, 2 = Mon, 3 = Tues, 4 = Wed, 5 = Thur, 6 = Fri, 0 = Sat)

Some of the alternative methods involve a smaller number of steps to be followed, but to compensate for this they either make heavier demands upon memory or require the user to consult printed tables. For example, with one method, to find the day of the week for any date in 1985 it is first necessary to memorize this twelve-digit number:

144025036146

Each digit represents the date of the first Sunday of one of the months in the year, ordered in sequence. Thus the first Sunday in January falls on the first, the first Sunday in February falls on the fourth, and so on.

With this information, provided one can subtract by sevens it is a fairly simple matter to find the day of the week for any date in that year. Thus, if I need to know the day of the week for 19 November, 1985, the memorized number tells me that the third of that month falls on a Sunday. Therefore the tenth and the seventeenth must also be Sundays, and the nineteenth, being two days afterwards, will be a Tuesday.

What happens if the date falls in a different year? The system would not be at all efficient if it was necessary to remember an entirely different twelve-digit number for every single year. Fortunately, this is not required. Because of the fact that there is a limited number of configurations of days within a month, all that is necessary is to take the same twelve-digit number and, for most years, follow the extra step of adding a number to the digit denoting the month in question. Within any year, the same number is added to the digit representing each month. Since there are seven days in each week, counting follows the base 7 number system, so that adding 1 to 6 brings us back to 0.

So, to calculate the day of the week for 19 November 1985, I consult the appropriate table, which tells me that the adjustment digit is 1. Next, I add this number to the digit for November in the twelve-digit list (which is 4), making 5. I then proceed as before: the first Sunday of that month is the fifth, so the second Sunday is the twelfth and the third Sunday is the nineteenth. Hence 19 November 1985 falls on a Sunday.

Note that the ways in which the above two alternative methods lead to correct answers to questions about calendar dates are not fundamentally different. The second method involves a smaller number of stages than the first but it necessitates taking the additional step of either consulting a table to ascertain the number by which each of the figures in the twelve-digit sequence should be adjusted for any particular year, or memorizing the adjustment figures for a sequence of years. There are other published ways to do calendar calculations but all are reasonably similar to one another. They demand varying amounts of attention to the different sub-tasks, that is, memorizing lists, consulting tables, memorizing different steps in the task, subtracting by sevens, and doing other calculations.

In principle, there is nothing particularly difficult about following any of the sequences of instruction. In practice, however, most people find the task tedious and time-consuming, even after a fair amount of practice. It is not surprising that calendar calculating has not caught on as a popular pastime: it would be hard to think of a more boring pursuit. In my own experience it is not much fun, to say the least!

Are the procedures by which retarded savants perform calendar calculations similar to the ones I have described? In most cases they probably are not. One reason for saying this is that it is hard to see how most retarded savants would actually encounter the information that is given in the published descriptions of methods for calendar calculating. It is just conceivable that some retarded people could independently arrive at methods similar to the published ones, but if they did so it would be difficult to explain another finding, which is that at least some (and possibly most) of the retarded savants who do calendar calculations are able to answer calendar questions that cannot be solved by using any of the methods I have described. For example, a well as being able solve problems which take the form: 'On what day of the week is the —— of —— in the year —— ?', a number of savants can readily answer other kinds of calendar query, such as, 'On what years does the —— of —— fall on a —— ?'. None of the published methods which I have encountered would be much help with a question like this one.

What aids, if any, have been available to retarded savants? A few have used so-called 'perpetual' calendars. These are devices which incorporate calendar rules and quickly direct the user to the particular configuration of days in a month that is appropriate for the date required. (Such devices are not truly perpetual, in fact; they typically cover several hundred years.) In some perpetual calendars the data are arranged on two rotating discs, providing a convenient means of finding the information required. In several instances it is clear that using perpetual calendars has helped people to acquire their calendar skills. In certain other cases retarded savants have taken very great interest in conventional calendars.

There may have been instances in which perpetual calendars have been available to retarded savants without the person investigating the case being aware of it. Louise LaFontaine (1974) has raised the possibility that a *World Almanac*, which contains a perpetual calendar, might have been available to the residents of certain state institutions in the USA. She also points out that a book entitled *Open Highways*, one of a series of children's readers published by Scott Foresman Ltd contains a perpetual calendar, outlined in yellow. She suggests that this might conceivably account for the fact that one mentally retarded calendar calculator who she studied reported, when asked to explain how he answered calendar questions, that he had 'yellow cards' in his head.

But it remains doubtful whether any retarded savants have had the opportunity to make use of the published methods for undertaking calendar calculations. It is hard to see how a mentally handicapped person would have been able to gain access to the available published instructions. A large proportion of retarded calendar calculators have been completely illiterate; those with some reading skills are unlikely to have possessed either the knowledge or the experience necessary to search through published sources, or to be able to follow the somewhat complicated verbal instructions provided. Nor are retarded people likely to encounter by change the kinds of books in which appropriate instructional information is given. Published descriptions are fairly easy to find, but only if the searcher has some expertise in making use of printed information. Mentally retarded people are virtually always at a disadvantage in this respect.

FOUR STUDIES OF CALENDAR EXPERTS

In the remainder of this chapter four relatively thorough investigations of calendar calculating in mentally retarded people are described. Each investigation made a serious attempt to understand the mental operations that underly calendar skills. The first of the four concerns a pair of twins; each of the others describes one individual person. I was personally involved in one of the investigations, which was undertaken by Julia Smith and myself.

Charles and George

The calendar calculating skills of a pair of retarded identical twins

103

named Charles and George were first described in two journal articles by William Horwitz and his colleagues (Horwitz *et al*. 1965; Horwitz, *et al*. 1969). The twins (strictly speaking, two surviving triplets; the third, a girl, having died within twelve hours of birth) were twenty-four years old at the time of the first report, but it was known that one of them, George, had possessed a talent for solving calendar problems since the age of six.

Charles and George had a difficult childhood. Their father was a violent alcoholic who sometimes struck his wife and children. There were two older sisters, both of normal intelligence. Both sisters trained as nurses and subsequently married. During the period when their mother was pregnant with Charles and George the father was drinking excessively, and throughout her pregnancy the mother was upset and she frequently vomited. After haemorrhaging at six months she was taken to hospital, where she gave birth to the triplets by caesarian section. Charles and George spent the first two months of life in incubators: when they were first taken out they both had convulsions. Subsequently the twins appeared to be healthy, but family life went on being stormy, with fighting between the parents and talk of divorce.

The babies were not difficult and in their first year they both appeared to be fairly normal, although Charles lagged behind George. But neither twin learned to talk or walk until he was well over two. When they were aged three a paediatrician told their mother that both twins were mentally retarded. She took this news badly, and she repeatedly said that she wished to kill herself and the twins as well.

Despite the father's alcoholism and the severe family difficulties it caused, the parents played a major role in encouraging their sons to acquire calendar skills. The mother and the sisters made efforts to teach the twins numbers and letters, but it was very hard to hold their attention. Yet both parents were impressed when they noticed that George at age six would spend hours poring over the perpetual calendar in an almanac. They felt that the talent he was starting to display was some kind of compensation from God. In this respect their response to the twin's talent was not unlike the reaction of Harriet's mother to her child's musical abilities.

Soon afterwards their father bought the twins a silver perpetual calendar. George would play with it for hours at a stretch. His parents and his aunt helped by testing him with dates, and George was given praise and encouragement when he answered questions correctly. Charles, who was always more retarded than George, did not at this time show any interest in calendar caluclating. He became involved later, but he never matched George's most striking achievements.

At the age of nine the twins went to live in a residential home. Tests revealed that they suffered from poor eyesight, both being severely myopic. As children they were sometimes aggressive and destructive, but they became more co-operative when they got older. They displayed some other unusual skills: both had the odd habit of picking out their own shoes by smell, although neither of them performed particularly well on objective tests measuring the ability to detect smells. George also learned the Greek alphabet and could play tunes on the piano.

Their calendar feats, as reported by Horwitz, were remarkable by any standards. George's achievements appear to have been matched in only one recorded case (to be described later). George was said to have a range of at least 6,000 years. He could provide the correct day of the week for dates as early as 1590. Prior to 1582, at which time the changeover took place between the Gregorian and Julian calendars, he would give the wrong answer, but only because he did not know that during that year a calendar adjustment was made by simply eliminating ten days. (This was necessary because the calendar system established in 46 BC by Julius Caesar was based on the incorrect assumption that each astronomical year lasts exactly one quarter of a day over 365 days. By the sixteenth century the accumulated discrepancy caused by the slight difference between this figure and the actual duration of the astronomical year was big enough to interfere with arrangements for selecting the dates for religious holidays.) Because of the change, anyone wishing to calculate the day of the week for a date earlier than 1582 must make an adjustment to compensate for the ten missing days. Since George did not know that this had to be done, his answers to questions about pre-1582 dates always contained a constant error.

George's and Charles's skills with dates were not limited to answering calendar questions in the usual form: they could solve other problems as well. For instance, if asked to state the years in which 21 April was a Sunday they would immediately give the required dates (such as 1968, 1963, 1957, and 1946). In George's case he could provide answers going back at least as far as 1700. In reply to a question asking for the months in 2002 in which the first falls on a Friday, George again gave the right answers: February, March and November. Both twins could also supply the correct dates when they were given appropriate specifications, such as 'The fourth Monday in February 1993?' (the twenty-second), or 'the third Monday in May 1936?' (the eighteenth). Horwitz and his co-authors noted that the range of George's skill extended beyond that of known perpetual calendars. As was mentioned earlier, perpetual calendars are in fact not truly perpetual: the spans vary, and they usually cover no more than 400 years. George's skill extended forwards beyond the year 7000. According to Horwitz he could calculate dates for which there exists no calendar.

So far as Horwitz could tell, neither twin had any real idea of the steps that he followed when confronted with a calendar question. Phrases such as 'I know' and 'It's in my head' were all that patient questioning succeeded in eliciting. 'My mother taught me' was another common answer to queries about their skills. Neither twin did at all well at tests of simple arithmetic: each would make mistakes on simple addition and multiplication questions. But they could do arithmetical problems based on concrete dates, a fact which shows that they did possess some arithmetical skills. For instance, either twin, when told someone's date of birth, could state the number of weeks elapsing until the next birthday or since the previous one. Furthermore, George, who knew the birth date of some famous historical figures, could state how old they would have been if they were still alive.

In a second report, Horwitz described the findings of some further investigations of Charles and George (Horwitz *et al.* 1969). The twins were asked to give the dates for Easter, and it turned out that George could do this over a thirty-year span. (It was possible that he had gained the information from *The Book of Common Prayer* or another Roman Catholic prayer book.) The investigators gave George a table specifying the dates of Easter up to the year 2100, and they tested him two weeks later. On this occasion he provided correct dates over a span of two hundred years but he did make a number of mistakes.

The investigators were impressed with the sheer speed at which both twins replied to calendar questions. Responses were not timed (possibly because they were thought to be too quick for accurate timing to be possible), but both George and Charles were said to answer 'in a flash'. Horwitz considered that the speed of replies was sufficiently fast to preclude the possibility that the method underlying the twins' feats involved extensive use of calculations, and noted,

An impulse that comes to mind when one first hears of the performance is that the boys depend entirely on a formula for calculation of the day of the week for a given date. No such suggestion is tenable, we believe, in view of the speed of answer and in view of their complete inability to perform the necessary calculations, even with time. (Horwitz *et al*. 1969: 413)

Horwitz felt that some further insight into the calendar feats of George and Charles might be gained from disovering whether certain years or decades caused more difficulty than others. For example, if it was found that there were gaps in their skills, or if certain groups of years were especially easy or difficult, such evidence might help to locate particular dates that the twins were using as 'anchor' points. However, no particularly informative clues emerged from this exercise. In Charles's case, he gave correct answers for most twentieth-century dates and for about half the nineteenth-century dates on which he was questioned. Beyond that range he perfomed at around chance level. When he did not know the answer his stock reply was 'Sunday'! George, in contrast, made hardly any errors at all, and the distribution of his rare mistakes gave the investigators no real hints about the method he followed. In fact it was thought that a substantial proportion of his errors could have been caused by hearing problems. Failures on a number of years were remedied when the year was written on a card rather than spoken.

Horwitz and his colleagues made only limited progress towards discovering exactly how George and Charles managed to achieve their calendar skills. The opportunity to study a perpetual calendar almost certainly played a key role, but exactly what the twins learned from it is not clear. It is extremely likely that the twins did a considerable amount of memorizing. Again, however, precisely what they memorized and how they used this knowledge for calculating calendar dates is by no means certain. Also, the fact that the twins, especially George, received encouragement from other members of the family and were regularly tested on calendar dates was probably very helpful.

Horwitz and his co-authors concluded that George and Charles began by memorizing a conventional calendar. From noticing that each month begins where the previous one ends and using this information to tack months and (later) years together, George was somehow able, eventually, to master the full 400-year range. Once this had been achieved, dates beyond that range could also be calculated, by subtracting years in multiples of 400, since the 400-year cycle repeats itself. But we are a long way from knowing what were the precise feats of memorization that George embarked upon in order to learn the initial 400-year range. However it was done, it must have been an enormous task.

A postscript to the investigation by Horwitz and his colleagues was added by Bernard Rimland (1978). He mentions that the producer of a film about the twins (who were also written about in a popular article that appeared in *Life Magazine*) paid a graduate student named Benj Langdon to learn one of the available methods for doing calendar calculations. It was hoped that his experience might yield some information about the skills of George and Charles. In fact the experiment did not yield any resounding new insight into the twins' performance, but there was one fascinating outcome. Rimland narrates that,

> Despite prodigious practice on Langdon's part, he could not match the speed of the twins' operations for a long time. Suddenly he discovered he could in fact match the twins in speed. Somehow, quite surprising to Langdon, his brain had automated the complex calculations, had absorbed the table to be memorized with such effectiveness that now the calendar calculating skill was second nature to Langdon and he no longer had to go through the various operations. (Rimland 1978: 61–2)

The phenomenon of skills that initially require deliberate effort and conscious control becoming automatized is by no means unique to calendar calculating. But the above account may help us to understand why the investigators' patient attempts to get George and Charles to explain their procedures proved so completely fruitless. Perhaps the twins could have provided a more helpful description in the early stages when they were just beginning to learn how to calculate calendar dates. Of course, their inability to describe the mental operations underlying a highly practised skill is not simply a limitation imposed by mental handicap. Intelligent people can be just as unsuccessful at describing how they perform a highly practised skill, once it has become automatic.

Yet another postscript to the twins' case, and a very penetrating one, has been added by a clinical neurologist, Oliver Sacks (1985). Unlike Horwitz and his colleagues, Sacks preferred to quietly observe the twins rather than test them, and although he was unable to learn much about their techniques he discovered some important facts about the twins which the other investigators had failed to see. For instance, after watching their eyes as they solved difficult calendar problems he noticed that,

> their eyes move and fix in a peculiar way as they do this – as if they were unrolling, or scrutinising, an inner landscape, a mental calendar. They have the look of 'seeing', of intense visualisation, although it has been concluded that what is involved is pure calculation. (Sacks 1985: 187)

Furthermore,

> And if you ask them how they can hold so much in their minds – a three-hundred figure digit, or the million events of four decades – they say, very simply, 'We see it'. And 'seeing' – 'visualising' – of extraordinary intensity, limitless range, and perfect fidelity, seems to be the key to this. (Sacks 1985: 188)

In the course of his quiet, almost surreptitious, observations of the twins as they pursued their ordinary lives, Sacks was struck by their consuming interest in, and fascination with, numbers of all kinds. He already knew that as well as being able to perform calendar feats they had remarkable memories for digits, and yet seemed incapable of simple arithmetical tasks involving multiplication and division; but he gradually became aware that numbers had a strange importance in their lives. On the occasion when he was watching them a box of matches fell on the floor, and the matches spilled out. Simultaneously, they both said '111', and, a little later, one murmured '37'. When Sacks counted the matches he found that they numbered exactly 111. He asked the twins how they could have counted the matches so quickly, only to be told that they did not count them, but 'saw' them. And when Sacks asked about the reason for murmuring '37', the twins replied together '37, 37, 37, 111'. One can only speculate about the explanation of this bizarre incident, but it seems to indicate some unusual kind of direct awareness by the twins of numbers and their properties. Sacks, understandably baffled, suggested that the twins might have somehow been able to 'see' the properties, 'not in a conceptual, abstract way, but as *qualities*, felt, sensuous, in some immediate, concrete way' (Sacks 1985: 190).

On a second occasion Sacks watched and listened to the twins as they sat together, smiling and clearly enjoying themselves. As he listened, he heard a kind of dialogue in which one twin would say a six-digit number, and the other would nod and smile, appearing to savour the number, and then he in turn would say a six-digit number, which, this time, the first twin would appear to enjoy and appreciate. Sacks reports that the twins seemed to resemble 'two connoisseurs wine-tasting, sharing rare tastes, rare appreciations' (Sacks 1985: 191). After making a note of some of the digit sequences which gave the twins so much pleasure, and giving the matter a lot of thought, Sacks, who admits to having had something of a passion for brooding on numbers in his own childhood, searched through some old tables of logarithms, powers, factors and prime numbers, and confirmed a hunch, that all the numbers which had been mentioned in the twins' exchanges were in fact prime numbers. On the following day he returned to the twins' ward, armed this time with a list of primes, and quietly joined the twins as they continued their dialogue. After a few minutes Sacks joined in with a number of his own, a prime with eight digits. The twins looked at him, and there was a long pause, and then they both suddenly, and simultaneously, broke into smiles. As Sacks realized,

> They had, after some unimaginable internal process of testing, suddenly seen my own eight-digit number as a prime – and this was manifestly a great joy, a double joy, to them: first because I had introduced a delightful new plaything, a prime of an order they had never previously encountered; and, secondly, because it was evident that I had seen what they were doing, that I liked it, that I admired it, and that I could join in myself. (Sacks 1985: 193)

The twins pursued the game with enthusiasm, and Sacks reports that an hour later they were swopping what appeared to be twenty-figure primes. Sacks's reports tell us nothing directly about the twin's mental operations as they solved calendar problems, but his insights make it clear that they possessed some kind of rare ability to experience numbers and their properties very directly. It is more than likely that the twins' unusual numerical abilities, whatever the precise form they may have taken, made a vital contribution to their calendar skills.

Hill's study

Turning from the frustratingly inconclusive efforts by Horwitz and his colleagues to explain the feats of George and Charles, and the fascinating but still inconclusive light thrown on them by Sacks's observations, I shall now consider another study, by A. Lewis Hill.

One of Horwitz's suggestions was that examining the form of the errors that people make in calculating calendar dates might yield some insights into the underlying mental operations. Although this approach met with little success in the twins' case, it might prove more effective when applied to the investigation of other individuals. Another possibility is that measuring the length of time necessary for answering different calendar questions may give an indication of their relative difficulty, and thus provide clues to the method that is being followed. In Hill's investigation (Hill, 1975) measures were made of the time required for numerous calendar calculations.

The person studied by Hill was a man in his fifties who had entered a school for the mentally retarded at the age of six years. He was said to have congenital syphilis. His score on the Stanford-Binet IQ test was 54. As well as being able to do calendar calculations, the man (who Hill calls B) was known to have an extensive memory for birthdays and other dates. He also drew elaborate pictures of houses and he could play eleven musical instruments by ear. No information was available concerning the time at which he first acquired his calendar skills.

Hill tested B at a number of tasks designed to assess memory and imagery, but no evidence of unusual abilities emerged. B's responses to the first set of calendar problems set by Hill and his replies to Hill's enquiries indicated that he might have been using a system in which memorized key dates played a major part. To investigate this possibility, Hill asked a number of questions that were designed to ascertain whether B found some dates easier or harder than others. The first step involved testing B on 168 different dates, arranged so that there was one date per month for each odd-numbered year between 1919 and 1943. Each question was spoken aloud, and a measure was made of the time it took B to respond. If no answer was provided after two minutes, the experimenter went on to the next question. B correctly answered 80 per cent of the questions, the median time taken to respond being just under eight seconds. Hill found that in four of the fourteen years used in the tests all of B's answers were correct: each of these (1943, 1945, 1951, and 1965) was a year on which 1 January fell on a Monday or a Friday. The largest number of errors occurred for the years 1947 and 1969, both of which began on a Wednesday. Afterwards, when B was being questioned about the dates on which he had made errors he told the experimenter that in 1947 he had been 'framed' and unfairly punished. Note the interesting parallel between this remark and the statement by Harriet, recorded in Chapter 2, that her performance with calendar dates was worse for the year in which her father died than for the adjoining years. In both cases deficits in performance appear to be related to periods of time during which stressful events occurred.

Hill made out a further examination of B's responses in order to determine whether his errors or his times to respond to particular dates, or both, varied systematically with the different days in a week or the months within a year. There were some differences but they were not so striking or so consistent as the ones associated with different years. Taking the findings as a whole, Hill concluded that they offered no support for the suggestion that B's method was based upon counting forwards and backwards from a limited number of memorized key dates.

The next step was to test B on a further list of questions. Hill needed to have some data about the best and worst months, weeks and days of the week for previously untested years that began either on a Friday (for which the first stage of the investigation had revealed better than average performance) or on a Wednesday (B having performed poorly on years beginning with that day). On this occasion B's general level of performance was better than in the first session, despite the fact that Hill had deliberately chosen dates which he expected to prove difficult. On 91 per cent of the dates B's answer was correct, and his median time to respond was 3.7 seconds. Hill statistically analysed the findings to determine whether there was any consistent variability in performance between different dates, weeks or days. No statistically significant differences emerged. However, the previous finding that quicker correct responses were made for years beginning with a Friday than for years beginning with a Wednesday was repeated in the new data.

A number of tests was given in order to assess B's ability to do arithmetic. He was competent at simple additions, although he always used his fingers if the total was greater than ten. With subtraction sums his performance followed a pattern that we have seen in other retarded savants who do calendar calculations. When he was simply asked to subtract ordinary numbers, he appeared totally incapable. But if the subtraction problem was presented in a more concrete form, such as, 'If you have three apples and you give me two, how many do you have left?', he had no trouble at all with subtracting, so long as the numbers were less than ten.

The results of his investigation convinced Hill that certain of the explanatory suggestions that have been put forward to try to account for calendar calculating in retarded savants could be ruled out in B's case. First, Hill found no evidence for any kind of imagery. Second, B's limited arithmetical skills made it appear unlikely that he could do the high-speed calculations necessary for using a method in which calculations as such played a major part. So far as Hill could discover, B did not seem to have any particular system.

What other possible explanations remain? Hill concluded that B probably relied very heavily on sheer memorizing. He noted that in order to do this B would have needed to be able to sustain concentration over long periods. Since B had shown no difficulty in concentrating during long hours of testing, it seemed to Hill that B might not have found it particularly difficult to give prolonged attention to calendar information.

In the absence of contradictory evidence it seems quite likely that B depended heavily on memorization. Conceivably, memorization has played an equally important role in the feats of most or even all mentally retarded calendar calculators. But even if that is correct, some crucial questions remain unanswered. Most importantly, precisely *what* is memorized, and exactly how does a person make use of the remembered information when he or she is faced with a particular calendar problem? It seems very unlikely that B remembered the day of the week for every single date within his range. The information he memorized was probably supplemented by a certain amount of forward and backward counting. But when it comes to specifying with any precision the detailed steps underlying B's achievements, we cannot be at all sure.

Dave

The next investigation began when Julia Smith and myself decided to investigate the calendar calculating skills of a boy Julia (JS) encountered in a school for children with learning difficulties (Smith and Howe 1985, Howe and Smith 1988, and Howe 1989). Although I met and talked with the boy, and worked with JS on the various stages of the investigation, all the formal testing was done by her.

Dave (not his real name) was born in 1965 of relatively elderly parents, his father being a farm labourer. His age was fourteen at the time of our investigation. It is not entirely clear just when his retarded development became noticeable. Just before reaching the age of four he tipped a pot of boiling stew over himself. As a result he was critically ill and spent almost eighteen months in hospital being treated for severe burns. His parents believed that this traumatic experience was the cause of mental retardation but a medical practitioner had previously noted that Dave walked on his toes: this can be an early sign of autism or spasticity. Even now he still tends to walk on his toes, and leans forward and moves with an air of stiffness. On intelligence tests administered in early childhood his scores were 54 (Junior WISC, administered in 1971) and 52 (Standford-Binet in 1972). At fourteen he could read a little, his reading age on a standard reading test (the Daniels and Diack test) being 6.5 years. The pattern of his responses on the test showed that his reading skills had been acquired by recognizing whole words rather than by applying word construction rules.

Compared with the other children at the special school he attended during the period of our investigation, Dave was noticeably solitary and withdrawn. He rarely talked or initiated contact with the other children, and unlike the others he rarely tried to gain the teachers's attention. It was unusual for him to ask questions. Sometimes another child would deliberately irritate or tease him. On these occasions he could get angry and aggressive: once or twice he was uncontrollable. But JS quickly gained the impression that despite his being uncommunicative, Dave's seemingly stubborn way of behaving was often quite effective for manipulating the teachers into letting him get his own way.

With his withdrawn and solitary temperament, Dave was not always as co-operative as we would have liked him to have been. At times he simply refused to answer questions or engage in conversation. JS noticed that sometimes when she tried to talk to him he would seem not to hear her. Yet he would answer, maybe some minutes later, as though the question had only just been asked, although with only a word or two and without any expression or emotion. We often had the feeling that he was in another world: he would answer some questions as if just from politeness, without appearing to pay attention or show any interest, and all the time giving the impression that he would much rather return to his own inner thoughts. Dave's speech was not always easy to understand. The only times when he spoke at all fluently, or with any real emotion, were occasions when the things he said appeared to be generated entirely by what he was thinking about at the time, and bore no relation to what was going on in the environment around him. Sometimes he would shake with laughter at whatever was on his mind, although he hardly ever laughed at anything that happened in the world outside himself.

Dave's uncommunicativeness made it difficult to collect data on his skills. JS met him on over twenty occasions: about two-thirds of them formed the sessions that yielded the findings described in this account. Sometimes Dave would be quite happy to answer calendar questions but at other times he was unwilling to co-operate at all. On other occasions he would be friendly and helpful at first but after a time – which could be as little as a few minutes or as much as half an hour – he seemed to become bored or restless. On the days when Dave's performance deteriorated in the course of a session it was not always immediately clear whether the drop in his level of success was caused by his experiencing real difficulties or by him becoming less willing to attend to our questions. For reasons like this it was not usually possible to specify in advance the exact contents of a particular session: a sequence of questions would be prepared but until the session was under way there was no knowing how many of them Dave would try to answer.

A problematic side-effect of Dave's unreliable co-operativeness revealed itself when we tried to use measures of the time that he took to respond to different kinds of questions. We had hoped to make use of his response times as indications of the varying difficulty of calculating different calendar dates. Unfortunately, it rapidly became clear to us that Dave's taking a long time to respond to a question was no guarantee that he needed a long time to reach the answer. On some occasions during the early sessions, when he had failed to respond to a question after a minute or two and was then given a reminder, he would the say the correct answer, instantaneously. It was obvious that Dave's failure to respond earlier was not necessarily an indication that the calculation had not been finished: just as likely, Dave had done it some time before but had forgotten or neglected to report the answer. Hence we could never take it for granted that response times accurately reflected the length of time Dave required to reach the answer to a calendar question.

Like other mentally handicapped people who do calendar date calculations, Dave was extraordinarily good at remembering birthdays. He could recall hundreds of dates given to him by children and staff at the school he attended. When we asked him factual questions about calendars he correctly stated the number of days in a week and the days in a month, but he surprised us by being unable to say the number of months in a year. So far as we could tell he had started to do calendar calculations at the age of nine years, and when asked how he answered calendar date questions he replied, reasonably enough, 'Use me brain'. If he was asked whether he followed a particular method that we described to him, or used any procedure we suggested, he would almost always reply, somewhat uninformatively, in the affirmative.

We realized from the outset that in order to progress beyond the achievements of earlier investigators it would be essential to confront Dave with a range of calendar problems, and ask him several different kinds of questions about dates. When we began to investigate Dave's abilities we had very few definite ideas about the possible nature of the skills underlying his calendar feats. Some of the tests we devised were designed to find out whether or not he was following methods similar to those that a person of normal intelligence would use to do calendar calculations, or particular steps contributing to the feat. We did not think that this was particularly likely, but in the absence of alternative suggestions it seemed sensible to find out whether or not we could rule out the possibility that Dave was using such methods. We also felt that it would be worth pursuing Hill's strategy of discovering which kinds of questions were easiest to answer and which ones caused more difficulty. Otherwise, we conspicuously lacked any detailed ideas or hypotheses about the way Dave arrived at the answers to questions about calendar dates.

We started by giving Dave a number of tests to find the limits of his calendar skills. First, a list of thirty-two dates was prepared, two for each decade for the years between 1900 and 2060. We simply asked Dave, 'On what day of the week is the —— of —— ,—— ', and recorded the answer and the time he took to respond. These questions gave him little difficulty: he gave thirty correct answers and made only two errors. On dates between about 1930 and 2000 he normally responded within ten seconds, but the more distant dates tended to need longer response times: for dates before 1930 or after 2400 the time to respond was always ten seconds or more. Sometimes Dave spontaneously added comments: for instance he said things like, 'I'll be X years then', or 'You'll be Y years old'. Remarks like these ones showed us that Dave had at least moderate competence at adding and subtracting, despite the fact that his teachers had told us he could not do arithmetic.

116

To find Dave's limits at answering straightforward calendar questions we next tested him on a wider spread of dates, ranging from 1850 to 2120. He again did well on days in years between 1900 and 2000, but for earlier and later dates his performance declined to chance level. There was some variability in his level of competence on different occasions: the first time he was tested on dates between the years 2000 and 2060 he answered eleven questions correctly out of twelve, but in a second session he correctly answered only three-questions out of six. If the same question was asked on different occasions Dave seemed to find it easier at the second attempt. The outcome of repeating eight questions on successive days appeared to confirm this, since for seven of them the response time was shorter on the second occasion. But since we had inadvertently chosen questions for which the initial time to respond was longer than average, the possibility of a regression effect cannot be ruled out.

The next step was to assess Dave's ability at subtracting. As I have already said, the indications we gained from some of his own comments seemed to be at variance with Dave's teachers' somewhat negative estimates of his arithmetical abilities. In fact, we found that when the questions we asked him were ones that were about calendar dates, he did relatively well. For example, it took him only three seconds to give the right answer to the question, 'If I was born in 1954, how old would I be in 2061?' He also correctly answered a fairly difficult problem of mental subtraction: 'If I was born in 1841, how old would I be in 2302?' He made only two mistakes in answering fourteen questions of this type. But when we asked him essentially the same subtraction questions in a form that was not so directly related to the elements of calendar date tasks, he was completely at sea. For instance, to 'What is 1981 minus 1963' he first said '9000' and later '3'. As with other retarded savants, it made the world of difference if dates were involved in the subtraction tasks he was given.

Dave was more successful at conventional subtraction tasks when they were easy ones, like 28 − 7, or 31 − 9. He answered each of fourteen such questions correctly. We had inserted into three questions several which involved subtracting 7 from another number. We had decided to do so because as most methods for calendar calculating necessitate subtracting by sevens at some point, we felt that superior performance by Dave at subtracting by sevens would give a positive indication that the operations followed by him included such subtractions. However, our findings produced no evidence at all of greater

117

fluency on Dave's part with subtractions that involved sevens than with those that contained no sevens.

Our next step was to look at Dave's mistakes. We thought that if there existed any consistent pattern in the errors he made, this might tell us something about the procedures he followed. When we classified Dave's errors on the basis of the number of days by which (incorrect) responses missed being correct, we did see a definite pattern, as is shown in the following data:

Number of days ahead of correct day	1	2	3	4	5	6
Frequency of errors	5	6	7	6	7	24

It is clear that Dave's wrong answers are by no means inaccurate by random numbers of days. In the fifty-five incorrect answers, he misses being correct by only one day on no less than twenty-nine of them. How can we explain this? One possibility is that many of the errors are cause by a failure to take leap years into account. Another possible explanation is that they could be due to misinformation about the number of days in a particular month. When we first realized that Dave's mistakes, far from being random, showed such a remarkable consistency, we were convinced that they would tell us a great lead about how he did calendar calculations.

After much further reflection we are not so sure. If we had possessed a much larger collection of errors, enabling us to undertake an analysis that involved examining the distribution of errors between different days in the week, and different months, years and decades, it might have been possible to get some clear answers. But the total number of errors we had available for examination was only fifty-five, and once these are divided into different days, months and so on, the numbers in each sub-group become too small to permit any clear deductions to be made. Of course, this problem could have been overcome by obtaining a much bigger sample of errors, but in practice it would have been very difficult to do so. Since Dave made relatively few mistakes (except in those years on which he was nearly always wrong, making the data useless for the current purpose) it took a substantial number of sessions to provide the fifty-five wrong answers that we did obtain. Bearing in mind Dave's unreliable co-operativeness we doubted whether the difficulties that would be involved in gathering a much larger collection of errors would have been justified.

From the limited amount of error data that we did succeed in obtaining, we were left with the feeling that the clear consistency of the mistakes probably indicates that they were caused by Dave being misinformed about some kind of calendar information, rather than by him simply making careless slips, but we are still not at all clear just why Dave was so often just one day out. It is interesting that the blind girl calendar date calculator described earlier was also prone to making errors that were just one day off the correct date. In her case the pattern of mistakes was definiteliy consistent with the possibility that she simply failed to take leap years into account. A similar explanation may well account for many of Dave's near misses.

For the next stage of the investigation we decided to confront Dave with questions that were quite different in form from the ones that asked for the day of the week on which a particular date falls. The questions which Dave was now required to answer included ones like, 'In what years does 9 October fall on a Wednesday?' One of the reasons for introducing problems of this kind is that Dave's responses would tell us whether or not we could completely rule out the possibility that he was following certain of the methods that can be used for solving calendar date problems.

The calendar calculating methods outlined earlier are effective for finding the correct day of the week for a given date, but they seem to be much less helpful for answering different kinds of questions, such as the ones that start with 'In what years. . .?' Moreover, if a person who performs calendar calculations is relying heavily on memory for large numbers of particular dates that function as 'bench marks' or 'key dates' or 'anchors' (as in the instance of someone who can say the day of the week for 27 December 1984, because she already knows that 25 December falls on a Tuesday, and simply adds two days to arrive at the correct answer, Thursday), the likelihood of her getting the correct answers to 'In what years . . .?' questions would seem to be small. Hence if Dave *can* deal effectively with various calendar problems that are quite different from the ones that ask for the day of the week for a particular day, it would appear that the method which he does follow, whatever it may be like, is neither at all similar to the calendar techniques we have already described, nor is it heavily based on the memorization of large numbers of particular key dates.

We were surprised how easily Dave answered questions that asked him to list the years on which a given date fell on a particular day of the week. He answered at a fast rate, and JS observed that there was a definite pattern in the intervals between his responses. Typically, he would pause at first, and then say about three (correct) years with no delay at all. Next there would be another slight delay, and then several more responses without any pause. His pauses usually occurred at the ends of decades.

Dave's impressive success at dealing with problems in this form offers no support at all for any suggested explanation that makes the assumption that he depended upon a method similar to one of the ones we have described. Nor does it lend support to the idea that memorized key dates are the major component of the procedure he followed. A quite different kind of explanation appears to be necessary. Dave's striking fluency at listing the years that have certain specified qualities suggested to us that his mental activity, at some stage, took the form of him 'reading off' correct responses, possibly from some kind of visual image.

We wondered if it was possible that Dave could have had access to an organized body of knowledge, perhaps conveyed via a visual image, about the ways in which the days in each month are actually arranged in a calendar. As it happened, JS had noticed at an early stage in the investigation that even while she was talking to Dave he would sometimes be drawing numbers, and when she looked more carefully at what he was doing she found that he was writing down dates as they would appear on each page of a monthly calendar. When he had completed a page it showed the days in a month, arranged as in a commercial calendar. (For an example of his drawing, see Figure 1.) When JS mentioned Dave's calendar drawing to his teachers she was told that he often did this: he seemed to enjoy drawing calendars. After reflecting on his unusual activity, it was hard to resist the conclusion that Dave's interest in the form and arrangement of the days within calendar months might be crucial to his calendar skills.

From observing Dave drawing calendars and questioning him about them, some interesting points emerged. First, the calendars he drew appeared to be copies of particular calendars he had seen. This is apparent in a number of ways: from symbols he inserted at the beginning of a month, which presumably had originally referred to the state of the moon and/or to tide positions; from the manner in which two dates were sometimes inserted in one position (see Figure 1); and from the way in which within each of the particular calendar months he drew the different representations of each digit are remarkably similar in form and size, whereas from one month to another the depiction of particular digits varies a great deal.

For example, in some of the calendar months drawn by Dave

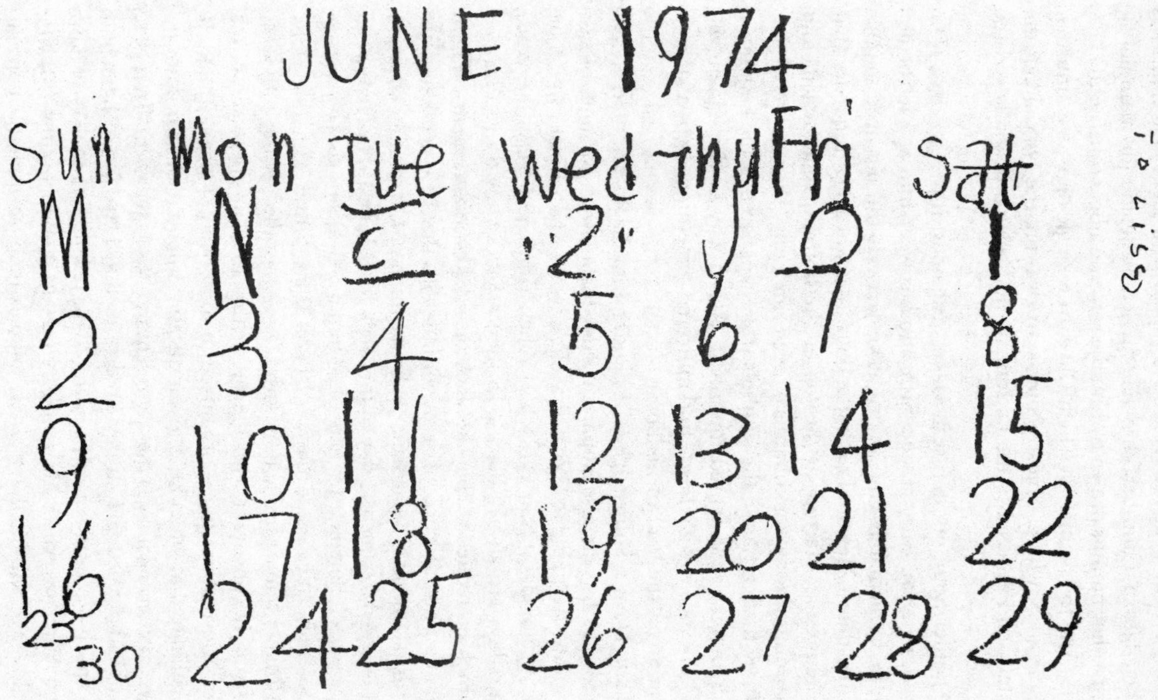

TO LISA

JUNE 1974

Sun	Mon	Tue	Wed	Thu	Fri	Sat
						1
2	3	4	5	6	7	8
9	10	11	12	13	14	15
16	17	18	19	20	21	22
23	24	25	26	27	28	29
30						

Figure 1 Calendar drawn by a mentally handicapped boy

certain numbers, such as 2s, always appear with serifs (the short lines at the edges of a number, drawn at an acute angle to the main digit), but in other months drawn by him the same numbers consistently lack serifs. And the manner in which Dave drew single digits was unusual. For instance, whereas most people start drawing the symbol 2 at the top left, and proceed to the bottom right, Dave consistently did the reverse.

Another point of interest in Dave's calendar drawing is that if he was asked at an early stage which number went into any particular box, he immediately gave the right answer. He did not need to refer to other dates. He could fill in the days in any order or sequence that was requested, starting at the top or the bottom, right or left, and proceeding via rows or columns or even randomly. We discovered that he knew that certain of the symbols which appeared at the beginning of his months represented the moon. Asked why he drew them, he said 'They always go there', and muttered something about a kitchen calendar on the wall of his home.

That Dave's knowledge of calendar months contributed to his calendar skills was also apparent from his answers to some of our questions. Replying to 'What day of the week was 6 April 1939?', he said, 'Thursday, that's black'. When JS asked why, he said, 'Thursdays are always black'. JS then asked, 'How do you know', to which he replied, 'They're black on my kitchen calendar'. These statements are clearly consistent with the idea that he was making use of a visual image of a particular calendar month. On another occasion he was asked to state the day of the week for 3 June 1956. He replied that it was a Thursday. JS then asked him if he was sure that his answer was correct. 'Yes', said Dave. 'It's on the top line.'

All these remarks, together with Dave's month-drawing activities, are strongly consistent with the suggestion that his approach makes use of information that is organized in some kind of visual image. It seems likely that when he is given questions about calendar dates he draws upon visual images that represent months as they actually appear in particular calendars. It occurred to us that Dave might have had the capacity to produce *eidetic images*. This term refers to very precise memory images which are made by certain young children (usually of below-average intelligence). It enables them to remember visual items in considerable detail, in a matter which is broadly congruous with the concept of 'photographic memory'.

Eidetic imagery is an odd phenomenon. Although it was confidently described in a number of early studies, careful research in recent years has found it to be somewhat elusive and not at all easy to measure or even to identify with any certainty (Haber, 1979). An added complication is that while it is reasonably certain that some children are capable of eidetic imagery, in the majority of cases it is doubtful whether the ability fulfils any practical function for the child concerned.

We decided to do a simple test in order to see whether Dave had any of the peculiar visual skills found in those children who are described as having eidetic imagery. A table was drawn up containing twenty-eight squares, roughly in the form of a calendar month, in which the numbers 1–8 were inserted, arranged at random. This was shown to Dave, and he was instructed to look at the table until he felt he 'knew' the contents. After about four minutes he said he did. He was then given an exact copy of the calendar frame in which the numbers had appeared, and asked to insert the original numbers in the appropriate positions. He rapidly wrote the correct numbers in the first two columns of the top line. At that point he paused, and after a short delay he supplied the number in the fifth column of the third row. Then he stopped, and said he could remember no more.

Despite our failure to show that Dave had the ability to form eidetic images, Dave's performance at calendar tasks and some of the remarks he made encouraged us to continue believing that visual imagery played a part in his calendar feats. We speculated that at some point in the procedures he followed, Dave was able to summon an image of a particular calendar month, giving him instant access to the day of the week for any date in that month.

It would be useful to be able to say exactly what a person has to know in order to 'know' a month, in the sense of having available in memory some kind of concrete representation (presumably image-based) of the configuration of dates forming a particular calendar month. In fact, for most of the days that form a month there are only seven possible configurations, each of which specifies how the days forming a month are arranged, since the first of the month can be on one of only seven different days, and the remaining days must follow accordingly. If a person has succeeded in committing to memory visual representations of each of the seven different configurations, and if (but it is a big 'if') that person is able to discover which of the seven configurations is the appropriate one for a particular date, then the memory image will readily direct that person to the correct answer.

I should emphasize that there is no definite evidence that Dave worked along these lines. Even if he did so the problem of ascertaining how he was able to specify which type of configuration was the appropriate arrangement for a particular month remains a daunting one, despite the fact that the different arrangements of days into months go in cycles, and are not chosen arbitrarily. But we decided to pursue some enquiries aimed at confirming or disconfirming the claim that Dave's approach depended on him retaining information about whole months as cohesive single units. It certainly seemed to be the case that whenever he was asked for a date he would produce the appropriate image, and then 'read off' the required day, just as if he was reading from a calendar.

JS started by asking Dave to say which month in each year started on a Friday. A person who has an image for every month ought to find it moderately easy to do this. With little apparent difficulty Dave ran through the correct months in every year from 1970 to 1990, and he gave the impression that he would have continued further had it not been necessary for JS to stop him because time was running out.

The next question was more crucial. JS gave Dave a list of seven months falling in particular years, as follows:

January 1971
September 1972
June 1973
July 1974
February 1971
August 1975
October 1976

In the above list, all of the months but one (February 1971) started on a Friday, but Dave was not told this. He was simply asked, 'Which of these is the odd one out?' We did not tell him anything at all about the kind of difference he was expected to look for. All the same, with very little hesitation he gave the correct answer, 'February 1971', and when JS asked him why he chose that month he said that he did so because, unlike the others, it started on a Monday.

Note that the question put to Dave said nothing at all about the start of the month. The question did not specify the form of the answer required: it merely indicated that Dave should look for some (unspecified) kind of difference. In fact the question provided no clue at all about what he was to look for. So far as we could tell, only by being able to conceptualize the structure of the entire month within which each date appeared could Dave have arrived at the right solution. Nevertheless, he did answer correctly. Dave's response to this question strengthened our belief that he was making use of some kind of knowledge about the characteristics of each month as a whole. This finding made it seem even more probably that he was drawing on a knowledge of the *appearance* of each calendar month. How, otherwise, could he have discerned what it was about the one month that was different from the others?

If Dave's method really did involve conjuring up an image of one month at a time, any error he made would indicate that he was using the wrong configuration for dates in that month. In that case it would be expected that a second question about a date in the identical month and year would elicit another wrong answer. However, if the next question following an error referred to a different month in the same year, then Dave would have to draw upon a different configuration. In that case we might expect the probability of him responding incorrectly to such a question, following an error on the previous question, to be no higher than the probability of him making an error following a previous correct answer.

To investigate this, in one of the sessions whenever Dave made an error JS would immediately (without telling Dave he was wrong) ask for other dates in the same month, and the dates in adjoining months. It was difficult to obtain a substantial amount of appropriate data, because since Dave usually made less than one error in every seven dates, and because following each error it was necessary to give him four subsequent questions about days surrounding that date, he had to be asked at least eleven questions, on average, to get each set of the results we required. Since Dave's concentration declined fairly rapidly in the course of a single session, it took JS two complete sessions to provide a small and not entirely conclusive body of data.

We found that following five out of six of Dave's wrong answers one or more of two subsequent questions about dates within the same month elicited further wrong answers. This finding does seem to support the view that Dave was using remembered configurations of specific calendar months. However, when following a wrong answer we switched to a question concerning a date in an adjoining calendar month, Dave's answers were again wrong in three instances out of six. So it would seem that shifting to another month does not immediately 'clear the deck' so far as Dave's method is concerned. This further finding would appear to suggest either that, contrary to our theory, Dave was not in fact drawing upon a memory image of the arrangement of the days within a particular month, or that, if he was doing so, the different configurations for adjoining months were not retained independently of one another.

Of course, the configuration of each month is *not* independent of the arrangement of the days in the preceding month. And it would have been useful for Dave to have been able to draw upon memorized configurations that were not of separate single months, but of *cycles* of months. Unfortunately, however, although it is interesting to speculate about the detailed nature of the retained calendar knowledge that Dave was able to draw upon, we rapidly reach the point at which such speculations run far beyond the empirical data that is available.

It then occurred to us that if Dave was making use of memorized images of the arrangements of days within particular single months, Dave could to all intents and purposes ignore the fact that not all months have thirty-one days. In that event, when he was asked about 'impossible' dates (for example, 31 September 1977) he might simply conjure up an appropriate image for the month and then read off the day, exactly as he would have done for a thirty-one-day month. There would be no particular reason for him to notice that the date was an impossible one. But the findings of a brief enquiry showed that Dave did not act in this way. When he was given questions that included impossible days he did not immediately say that no such day existed, but he responded as if he was progressing with his customary procedures, until he reached a point at which there appeared to be some kind of obstacle. He then appeared worried and reported, quite rightly, that there was no such day. It appeared that the method which he was following did not immediately reveal to him that the day did not exist, and that this knowledge eventually became apparent to him, but at a relatively late step in his sequence of operations.

Looking at this investigation as a whole, it has certainly raised a number of interesting suggestions about the mental activities that underlie Dave's achievements. In some respects it brings us closer than previous research has done towards being able to understand how one mentally retarded individual finds the answers to difficult questions about calendar dates. But it leaves many questions unanswered.

It is clear that if we were in a position to describe the form and content of Dave's calendar knowledge in precise detail we would advance a long way towards being able to state exactly how he answers calendar questions. Like Charles and George, Dave definitely knows a great deal about calendars, but unlike them his knowledge comes from conventional calendars rather than 'perpetual' ones. (We should not make too much of this distinction: Charles and George did use conventional calendars as well as perpetual ones, and, of course, the two types of calendar are inevitably very similar in many respects.)

As with most (but not all) retarded people who do calendar calculations, there is fairly convincing evidence that Dave experiences some form of visual imagery: some of his answers to questions suggest that he makes considerable use of such imagery. In that respect he is not unlike the handicapped young man who would regularly gaze at the ceiling before responding to calendar questions; but he is very different from the girl who performed calendar feats despite being blind since infancy. However, the question of how Dave manages to produce the *right* image on a particular occasion is far from fully answered. Perhaps, at a relatively late stage in the sequence of his mental operations, he summons a visual image representing the correct configuration of days in a particular month. But we simply do not know how the images for different months are related to one another within the structure of Dave's knowledge.

There are many gaps in our understanding of the content, form and organization of whatever Dave knows about calendars. We are not clear whether his knowledge takes the form of a single, very tightly organized body of integrated information, or whether he draws upon a large number of separate memory records that (for him) form unrelated pieces of information. The findings we have encountered would seem to rule out either of these two extremes, but precisely how organized his knowledge about calendars is, and exactly what are the principles underlying such organization, we simply do not know.

One fact that emerges very clearly from the investigations we have described up to this point is that individual calendar calculators do not all work in the same way. For instance, as we have seen, some people definitely appear to rely heavily on visual imagery but others equally definitely do not. Dave acted as if he 'saw' monthly calendars when he was given a problem; the twins also appeared to 'see' numbers; but Hill's subject provided no evidence that he was making use of visual images. And although the ability to memorize large amounts of detailed information is almost certainly essential for all retarded calendar calculators, the centrality of memorization as such differs considerably from one individual to another.

In Chapter 3 we asked how mentally retarded individuals can be so good at memorizing, a task which most people find arduous and difficult. It was stressed that saying that somebody memorizes some information does not necessarily imply that the person deliberately sets out to memorize, or has a definite intention to do so. In normal and retarded people alike the intention as such is less important than whether or not the person attends to the information. The reason why we find it so difficult to memorize large numbers of dates is that it is unpleasant to sustain prolonged attention to something so boring as calendar dates. When we direct out attention to something that we find interesting we tend to remember it well. If we were very interested in dates, as some retarded savants seem to be, and if we gave calendars our attention for very long periods of time, we too would retain large quantities of information about calendar dates, even if we lacked any definite intention to memorize them.

In Hill's study, he came to the conclusion that his subject must have relied very heavily on sheer memorizing. Conceivably, the man may have based his performance upon a body of stored information about dates which he might have been able to remember even if he did not have much understanding of the manner in which calendar information is structured or of the principles by which calendars are formed. But in the case of other individuals such as Dave, and also the twins, it is clear that very extensive mental activity went into their calendar skills beyond whatever processing was required just for memorizing large numbers of dates. That is not to deny that considerable remembering has to be done by all retarded people who have calendar skills. Memorization is essential for all calendar feats but, at least for the most difficult ones, it is not sufficient.

Rodney

The final individual to be described in this chapter is a man who was more intelligent than the others: he was only mildly retarded. Rodney W. was in his late thirties when he agreed to co-operate with Brett E. Kahr and Ulric Neisser in a project they undertook in order to investigate his calendar calculating abiliies (Kahr and Neisser 1982). He led a semi-independent life in a sheltered home environment.

Kahr and Neisser asked Rodney to give the correct day of the week for each of a large number of dates. As in the investigation that A. Lewis Hill conducted, it was hoped that the pattern of differences in the times required to answer questions referring to various categories of dates would shed light on the methods that Rodney was using. Dates were written on cards, arranged in decks of fifty. Rodney was asked to look at the cards one at a time, saying the correct day of the week as quickly as possible. The clearest finding was that the questions which were arranged in decks containing items from a variety of different centuries took about three times as long as those in decks that were restricted to the present century. The effects of restricting the questions to one single year depended upon the particular year that was chosen. Rodney answered fifty questions on dates that were all in 1976 considerably faster than random dates within the twentieth century, but there was no such improvement with a sequence of fifty dates all taken from the year 1902. Decks of questions restricted to particular days or months in different years were answered no faster than sequences of random dates.

Interesting as these results are, they do not tell us a great amount about Rodney's methods. However, some of Rodney's own statements about the procedures he followed were quite informative. At first, he parried questions about the methods he followed saying, 'It's just a talent I've got'. But later he responded to the investigators' queries with some more interesting comments. For dates within his own lifetime, he claimed that he simply remembered the correct answer. He said that his knowledge was based on direct recall of each and every day since he was about four years old. He may have been right about this: on the other hand it has been shown that people's insights about when and where they acquired particular items of remembered information can be extremely unreliable.

Rodney's method for answering many dates in the twentieth century appeared to be based on the fact that he had memorized the day of the week on which his birthday fell in every single year. When he was asked about 20 May 1926, he explained (after giving the answer, Thursday, in less than two seconds) that since he knew that his birthday in that year was a Friday, he could easily calculate that 20 May, eight days earlier, was a Thursday. He also knew that calendar patterns of the days within a year repeat themselves in a twenty-eight-year cycle, and used this knowledge when asked about dates in the past, simply adding multiples of twenty-eight to the given year until he arrived at a year for which he already knew the calendar.

Rodney's answers for dates before 1582 were incorrect, simply because, like George, he did not know about the shift between Julian and Gregorian calendars. The fact that he made such mistakes provided Kahr and Neisser with partial verification of Rodney's own explanation of his procedures, since these errors would not have occurred if Rodney's performance with such dates had been based on memory for information about those years, taken from a conventional or perpetual calendar.

When Kahr and Neisser examined Rodney's actual response times they found that his responses were indeed faster for questions about years within the period which he claimed to 'know'. But they also suggested that, if Rodney's account of his procedures was accurate, for years before 1947 Rodney ought to be faster with recent than with earlier dates (because the required calculations are simpler) but that within the dates for which he claimed to draw directly upon his knowledge (thereby making calculating unnecessary) there should be no difference in response times in favour of the more recent years. Again, the actual findings did confirm Rodney's own account.

GENERAL CONCLUSIONS

To what extent does a knowledge of the methods utilized by one calendar calculator help us understand the processes followed by other people who perform similar feats? When Julia Smith and I began the examination of Dave's skills we were confident that discovering how one retarded savant managed to do calendar calculations would take us a long way towards knowing how all savants perform that feat. I no longer think this is true. The striking differences between the approaches of those calendar calculators whose skills have been investigated prove that the procedures followed by different individuals are exceedingly diverse. Undoubtedly there are similarities in the methods of different people, even if it is quite possible that no two retarded calendar calculators adopt identical procedures, and there are some common elements in the calendar skills of mentally retarded individuals (White 1988, Goldsmith and Feldman 1988).

Even so, certain similarities may be more apparent than real. In Rodney's case, we must not neglect the importance of his superior intelligence, compared with that of all the other people whose calendar skills have been studied. The majority of mentally retarded calendar experts are less articulate and unlikely to have been able to gain a comparable grasp of the principles of calendar construction. To discern that calendars repeat themselves and to appreciate the implications of this fact for calculating calendar dates demands a degree of conceptual understanding that people of lower intelligence than Rodney may lack. And it cannot be taken for granted that a mentally retarded individual will acquire the calculating skills necessary for adding and subtracting in multiples of twenty-eight.

Thanks largely to Rodney's own insights, the investigation by Kahr and Neisser succeeded in identifying some of the procedures followed by one individual who can perform calendar calculations. Some important questions about Rodney's skills remain to be answered, of course. For instance, it would be interesting to know how he originally gained his calendar abilities. It would also be interesting to know how he, or George, or B, would have dealt with the 'In what years does . . .?' kinds of questions that were posed in the study investigating Dave. My guess is that Rodney would not be as successful as Dave, who responded not only correctly but very fast, typically giving two or three years before each pause when replying to a question such as 'In what years is 3 March on a Wednesday?' To achieve this level of performance it is probably necessary to have some kind of representation of the physical arrangement of the days and months in a year. As I have already suggested, it would seem more likely that this can be achieved by having calendars represented in one's mind in the kind of form that we might associate with having mental images, than by relying on memory for particular dates, possibly supplemented by information about the principles of calendar construction. Dave clearly remembered how particular months were represented in a spatial calendar, as he demonstrated by his calendar drawing activities.

Apart from the importance of differences in people's intellectual capacities, differences in the way different people approach calendar tasks place limits on the likelihood of it being possible to make valid general statements about how calendar calculating is achieved. In the case of Dave, as we have seen, it appears likely that his skill depends upon an ability to form visual images. Imagery probably also plays a part in the feats of George and Charles. With B there is no way of knowing with any degree of certainty whether or not mental imagery is involved in his procedures. But it is unlikely that visual images contributed at all to Rodney's calendar feats. Kahr and Neisser tested Rodney's ability to use visual images as a memory aid by asking him to follow the steps of a well known mnemonic procedure, the *Method of Loci*. Very briefly, this involves telling a person to form images in which specified items are visualized as being present in locations that are already highly familiar. Subsequently, the person tries to recall the (imaged) object at each of the imaged familiar locations. Most people find it easy to follow this procedure, and have no difficulty in recalling ten or more objects. Rodney had no success at all: he could remember only one item out of ten. Of course, Rodney's poor performance at that level does not prove that he cannot use visual imagery; nor does it prove that imagery plays no part in his calendar calculations. Yet the balance of evidence suggests that imagery makes no real contribution to Rodney's calendar skills.

Despite all the uncertainties that remain, it is clear that a useful degree of demystification has been achieved. We cannot say that we know exactly how mentally handicapped individuals perform the feat of calendar calculating but, in certain cases at least, their skills no longer appear to be totally mysterious or inexplicable. There is nothing magical about the feats: they do not rely on strange mental powers that are entirely different from the cognitive skills of ordinary people. Retarded savants are different from ordinary individuals, of course, and they are also different from the majority of mentally retarded people. But the ways in which they differ ultimately depend more on features of temperament and personality that influence how they pass their time, how they direct their attention, and why they are not distracted by events which most people would find interesting, than on their having any extraordinary computing or memory powers. (Of course, being able to concentrate for long periods of time and avoid all distractions, especially personal ones, is even more profitable if one is not mentally retarded: Newton and Einstein were both remarkable in that respect.) If other achievements by savants are equally amenable to investigation it ought to be possible to acquire an increased understanding of the mental operations that underly a number of the feats they exhibit.

In this chapter much more has been said about *how* retarded savants become calendar experts than about *why* they do so. Except for speculation, there is little to add to the remarks that were made in Chapter 3. For some individuals, thinking about calendars may be a means to escape from unpleasant events or thoughts, or a way to avoid situations associated with failure, or to steer clear of difficult social encounters. Some time ago I talked to a mentally handicapped man in his sixties, who had been drawn to my attention by friends who knew of my interest in calendar calculating. It turned out that his calendar calculating skills were not very impressive, but he did have an uncanny ability to remember dates that were associated with important events in the lives of himself and the people he knew. For him, knowing about fixed dates seemed to be a way of having some kind of control in the midst of all the confusing events that life presented.

Although calendars do not strike most ordinary people as being interesting enough to repay sustained concentration, they are more likely to engage the attention of someone who is not excited by the things that are full of interest for most people. Most of us assume that everyone is interested in other human beings, but that is not quite true. For example, autistic individuals are not, probably because they cannot understand what it is like to be another person. In those circumstances calendars, and perhaps digit sequences as well, might appear to be considerably more worthy of attention than ordinary people like ourselves are able to imagine.

Chapter Six

MENTALLY HANDICAPPED ARTISTS

The art of mentally retarded people is often fascinating but until comparatively recently there has never been a case of a mentally retarded child or adult showing a talent for visual arts that is comparable to the most striking achievements of retarded savants in other spheres. That situation changed dramatically in 1977 with the publication of *Nadia*, a book which described a mentally retarded young girl whose drawings depicted real objects in the world with an accuracy that far exceeded even the best achievements of the most intelligent children.

Children are not good at reproducing the visual appearance of objects in realistic drawings and paintings. It has been said that they draw what they know rather than what they see. In fact this is a gross oversimplification but one which contains some truth. A child may draw something in order to send a message, or to entertain, or decorate, or even to express emotion, perhaps without much thought to depicting objects with strict visual accuracy, as they 'really' appear. A child's stereotyped drawing of a house demonstrates a knowledge of the way in which houses are usually drawn by other children: it follows the usual conventions, and is not always a serious attempt to evoke the appearance of a particular dwelling. Drawings communicate a child's knowledge that animals have four legs, that houses have doors, windows and chimneys, and so on.

One of the reasons why children's drawings are so poor at showing how things actually appear is that achieving this is not at all easy: it demands certain mental skills that are not acquired until early adolescence. Lorna Selfe, a psychologist, searched through many thousands of drawings and paintings by normal and retarded children without finding any instances in which the ability to represent objects was markedly ahead of the child's general intellectual development.

134

Figure 2 Typical children's drawings

Source: L. Selfe (1977) *Nadia: a case of extraordinary drawing ability in an autistic child.*

135

To all intents and purposes, young children simply *cannot* realistically reproduce what they see. Figure 2 shows some typical examples of children's art. The obvious limitations are virtually universal in human cultures. Lorna Selfe quotes from one of the first researchers to study the development of artistic abilities in the young.

> In spite of careful research the writer has been unable to locate a single child under the age of 12 years whose drawings appeared to possess artistic merit of a degree at all comparable with the musical genius occasionally shown by children of this age. (Goodenough 1926)

There have been a few interesting instances of mentally handicapped people whose artistic achievements have outstripped their other abilities. The eighteenth-century painter, Gottfried Mind, was a striking example. Born in Switzerland, Mind became famous for his lifelike drawings and watercolours of animals, and he was known as 'the Cats' Raphael'. The English King George IV acquired a picture by him, depicting a cat with its kittens. Yet Mind was a cretin, severely retarded, who had no idea of the value of money, could neither read nor write, and was incapable of earning a living at any ordinary occupation.

One of the rare reports of superior artistic abilities in a mentally retarded person describes a sixteen-year-old French boy, who had a mental age of six years, could not read, write or do numerical calculations, and knew only a few letters. He produced some interesting and very detailed townscapes, filled with small drawings of houses and other objects such as ships. His mother reported that the pictures came from his imagination, and were not copies of anything he had seen. In the drawings,

> Il y a un certain sens de perspective, mais d'une perspective qui rappelle celles des primitifs, les objets les plus lointains étant de la même grandeur and simplement placés au-dessus des objets les plus rapproches. De plus, nous observons un luxe de détails frappant: l'heure est indiquée à un clocher, une girouette représentant un ange casque est entièrement déssinée. On distingue des lampadaires sur les places et les bâteaux ne sont pas moins travaillés. (Stern and Maire 1937: 459)

Japan has produced several mentally retarded artists. Yoshihiko Yamomoto, who is reported to have been unable to reply to simple questions such as 'What is your name?', to have an IQ of around 40, and to resemble 'a Buddha statue in his ability to sit in his seat for an entire day', suggesting a possible diagnosis of autism, has produced many impressive pictures. Much of his art is based on printmaking techniques which the dedicated teacher who guided his earliest attempts at drawing encouraged him to learn. He can also paint with oils and water colours (Morishima 1974; Morishima and Brown 1976).

Kiyoshi Yamashita is another talented Japanese artist who is mentally handicapped. After an appalling early childhood he was placed in a home for retarded children. His IQ of 68 indicates that he is less severely retarded than many retarded savants. He works mainly in oil but has also produced paper montages. His work is highly regarded in Japan, as the following statement demonstrates:

> His artistic productions are considered exceptional by the high standards of critics. The press has called him the 'van Gogh of Japan' and a 'wandering genius'. However, Yamashita's other behavior remains at a primitive level. He wanders about Japan, begging for food and sleeping in railway stations. His face remains expressionless. His written compositions have a direct experiential style which, although more childish, is somewhat reminiscent of Joyce or Proust. (Lindsley 1965: 226)

A moving account of an artistically talented mentally retarded adult is given by Oliver Sacks, a clinical neurologist (Sacks 1985). So far as Sacks could discover, the man, named Jose, was quite normal until the age of eight, when severe brain damage occurred, accompanied by frequent violent seizures. Jose was left profoundly retarded, autistic, epileptic, and with no speech. Sacks, who met Jose on a number of occasions, describes how drawing (which Jose had enjoyed as a young child, encouraged by his father, who liked to sketch, and his older brother, who later became a successful artist) was the one capacity that remained intact. Many of his drawings are of natural objects – fish, birds and flowers, for instance. They are realistic, expressive and lifelike, displaying qualities that can never be seen in Jose's everyday activities. Watching Jose copying a magazine picture of a rainbow trout, Sacks observed,

> I smiled myself, involuntarily, as he drew it, because now, feeling comfortable with me, he was letting himself go, and what was emerging, slyly, was not just a fish, but a fish with a 'character'

of sorts. . . . The fish showed a lively and distinctive imagination, a sense of humour, and something akin to fairy-tale art. Certainly not great art, it was 'primitive', perhaps it was child-art; but, without doubt, it was part of a sort. And imagination, playfulness, art, are precisely what one does not expect in idiots, or *idiots savants*, or in the autistic either. Such at least is the prevailing opinion. (Sacks 1985: 209)

Artistic achievements resist the quantitative assessments that are possible with memory and calculating skills. Excepting Gottfried Mind's paintings, the degree of technical expertise at depicting realism in pictures by mentally handicapped people is rarely exceptionally high. Most of the work of these artists could be described as primitive art. It is hard to make direct comparisons between the talents displayed in their paintings and those of normal people.

Such a comparison is possible, however, in the case of one quite extraordinary child artist. The child and her work are the subject of a book, *Nadia: a case of extraordinary drawing ability in an autistic child*, by Lorna Selfe, published in 1977. This book is the source of the following description of Nadia's talents. What makes this particular case especially fascinating is that it is possible to state with certainty that there is no conceivable way in which any normal child of the same age could have equalled Nadia's achievements. With almost all the other savant feats it is true to say either that they can be done by at least a few people of normal intelligence or that, so far as one can tell, intelligent people could perform them if they were willing and able to devote a very large proportion of their time to uninteresting (and sometimes apparently pointless) tasks of learning or remembering. Nadia's feats present a rare exception. They are virtually unique, although the skills of one older boy, aged thirteen in 1987, who produces excellent drawings of buildings, may turn out to be comparable.

Nadia's talent was discovered in January 1974 when a woman brought to the Child Development Research Unit at Nottingham some pictures which she said had been drawn by her six-year-old daughter, Nadia. The pictures, drawn faintly in ballpoint ink on cheap paper, were mostly of horses, birds and other animals. They were astonishingly realistic, and so accurate, accomplished and lifelike that the psychologists who examined them found it hard to believe that they could possibly have been done by a six-year-old child. Lorna

Selfe and her colleagues at Nottingham did not lack knowledge about what is normally possible in child art. In fact, they had just finished analysing a collection of 24,000 'pictures of Mummy' that had been submitted to a competition for children. The skills displayed in the pictures which Nadia's mother was showing them were far in advance of anything that other children achieved.

Nadia was autistic. She did not respond to other people's social approaches. Often it was difficult to know whether her unresponsiveness to instructions and attempts to communicate with her was due to inability to understand or to an unwillingness to cooperate. She herself spoke hardly at all. Lorna Selfe observed her at least twice per week over a five-month period but she detected only ten separate single-word responses. Nadia's movements were very slow and clumsy, and she was unusually large for her age. Nadia's early family life had been unusual, but even as a young infant she was physically unresponsive to her mother. Abnormal language development was apparent by the time she was nine months old. These very early signs of autism suggest that her home background is unlikely to have been the main cause of Nadia's difficulties.

Nadia's parents, who came to Britain from the Ukraine in 1947, had three children. Nadia was the middle one. The others were bilingual and they developed normally. At the age of three Nadia was separated from her mother, who had to go to hospital with breast cancer. The child was looked after by her grandmother, who spoke hardly any English. But the signs of abnormality were beginning to multiply well before the separation took place. Nadia did not attend to people, she was very hard to control, and she gave the impression of being emotionally isolated from everyone else.

At the age of four-and-a-half Nadia entered a special school for subnormal children. Her behaviour there was described as being passive and slow, although at school and home alike she sometimes had uncontrollable temper tantrums, when she would scream for hours at a time. But usually she would sit staring into space or wander aimlessly around the room. Like a number of the children we have encountered in this book she was described by adults as seeming to withdraw into a world of her own. She rarely made contact with other children, but she was usually co-operative enough to show that she could understand simple instructions.

It was at school that Nadia's drawing ability was first noticed. She made almost no progress in acquiring language but she coped well

Figure 3 Drawing by Nadia

Source: L. Selfe (1977) *Nadia: a case of extraordinary drawing ability in an autistic child.*

Figure 4 Drawing by Nadia

Source: L. Selfe (1977) *Nadia: a case of extrarodinary drawing ability in an autistic child.*

141

with toys such as jigsaws, form boards and an apparatus for practising threading shoelaces, all of which can help promote perceptual and movement-based kinds of learning. She would persist at these toys until she mastered them. When the teachers discovered that she was good at drawing they encouraged her to develop her ability.

Figures 3 and 4 show some examples of Nadia's art. Some of them were drawn when she was as young a three years of age. They stand out in sharp contrast with the drawings of normal children that are shown in Figure 2. Lorna Selfe pointed out that Nadia's pictures, unlike those of other children, displayed an ability to represent perspective and proportion, the illusion of movement, and foreshortening, as well as impressive manual dexterity, Moreover,

> Her drawings . . . were marked by inventiveness and experimentation. . . . The techniques of perspective, foreshortening and the use of space were present from the age of three-and-a-half to four years, although perspective usually only develops in early adolescence. It is, in fact, often absent in the drawings of primitives and is regarded as one of the marks of sophistication of mature drawing. (Selfe 1977: 101)

The drawings of normal children, in contrast with Nadia's, tend to be schematic, rigid, and stereotyped. They typically contain numerous mistakes: for example legs and arms are depicted as being joined to the wrong part of the body, or all four legs of a horse are reproduced as being entirely visible.

Her paintings are not direct copies, but many of them seem to have been based on pictures – typically from children's picture books, newspapers or prints on the wall – which she had seen, perhaps a day or two earlier. The originals are generally recognizable in her drawings but are not reproduced in their exact form. The drawings are sometimes different in size, or the direction may be reversed. The following extract suggests that Nadia was by no means slavishly copying what she had seen:

> Her pictures of horses, for example, may have been a composite of the many horses she had observed and it was difficult to find originals since there were so many possibilities. In cases where the original has been found and where other sources can be safely ruled out we can seen that she frequently distorted and transformed the original but often to render her drawing more interesting. The

essential features and basic shape, however, were rarely destroyed, or so distorted as to leave the reproduction unrecognizable. A fascinating feature of her ability was that she paid attention to those features which normally receive most attention in the drawings of intelligent children – or in visual scanning – such as the face of the animal. (Selfe 1977: 10)

I think it is important to an understanding of Nadia's talent to know that she did not just look at the pictures which served as the originals for her drawings. She 'studied' them (to use Lorna Selfe's word) attentively, sometimes for long periods of time. While she did this she would occasionally scribble on the outlines. She certainly learned a great deal from paying close attention to the particular manner in which items are depicted in a drawing or a painting.

We know tantalizingly little about Nadia's mental activities during the time when she was gazing at pictures, before she started on a drawing. (Additional knowledge of her activities would doubtless provide some useful clues to ther drawing ability.) As she looked at a picture, she would almost certainly have been processing information about its physical dimensions – the lines, elevations, dimensions, angles, and so on. One is tempted to think that whereas a normal child who looks at a picture gives attention to the meanings of the visual display, and to whatever the picture represents or communicates, Nadia would have been preoccupied with the picture's physical structure. It might seem that Nadia was unaware of the picture's meaning, and therefore free to concentrate her mind on observing its form. But such a suggestion, however beguiling, is certainly an over-simplification: Nadia's paintings conclusively demonstrate that she did take account of the meaning of what she was drawing. Consider, for example, some of her drawings of cockerels (Figures 4). Note that Nadia's drawings include a tongue, although there was no tongue on the original picture. She must have 'introduced' a tongue, using what she knew about birds. This would have been quite impossible without some understanding of what the picture represented.

Yet although meaning did play a part in Nadia's drawings, her lack of language imposed sharp limits on her understanding of the visual world. Language makes a huge difference. In ordinary children, the fact that the seen world is conceptualized or restructured through language is a reason why their drawings and paintings are infused with conceptual knowledge. (A dog is drawn with four legs visible, for example.) A child's drawings may seem to tell us more about what is going on in the child's mind than about the visual appearance of the object. Lorna Selfe refers to Buhler's statement that the acquisition of language exercises a tyranny on the mind. She notes,

> It is ironic that many artists have claimed that one of the ultimate aims of art is to draw an object as it is perceived, uncontaminated by language or intellect. . . . Nadia, with her extreme impoverishment on both the language and intellectual side drew what she perceived. Like the camera, she recorded a footballer with a massive foot because this was extended towards the viewer – no allowance (and reduction) was made for what she *knew* about the size of the human foot in relation to the human body. (Selfe 1977: 126)

Nadia also produced drawings which give a very realistic impression of perspective, even though the animal is depicted from an angle which is quite different from that shown in the original. This would not have been possible if her special skill had rested only on her knowing how lines and angles are depicted in a picture. At the very least, Nadia must have gained some understanding of how the lines on a two-dimensional image can be made to represent a three-dimensional object. Perhaps she was able to form some kind of image of the three-dimensional object. She might then have been able to rotate the image in order to regard it from a different angle, and subsequently make a drawing that conveyed on paper the appearance of this 'new' three-dimensional object. But however she achieved it, there is nothing at all simple or easy about the feat of depicting in two dimensions a three-dimensional object in a manner that evokes how the original object actually appears. Much more than copying is involved. A two-dimensional picture has to give an illusion of a three-dimensional object.

When Nadia started to draw an object, she must have already had a clear image of it in her mind. It is possible that what she was doing as she drew was largely a matter of 'tracing' from such an image, and it is even conceivable that she was able to somehow 'project' a visual image on to the paper in front of her; but this is sheer speculation. That Nadia's painting activity could have taken the form of transferring some kind of image is suggested by the following extract from Lorna Selfe's description of her sequence of actions in depicting a horse's head. Nadia had not drawn this particular head before: so, Selfe argues, the possibility that her approach to this task depended on her having practised it can be excluded. Unlike most children and adults Nadia started with the neck, rather than outlining the head.

> Nadia then positioned the ears before drawing the rest of the head so that at one point she achieved the remarkable feat of having related the neck and ears in a correct special relationship without guidance from the lines of the head that were still to be drawn. (Selfe 1977: 14)

As well as being more realistic, Nadia's drawings differ in other ways from those of other children. For example, as Lorna Selfe points out, with normal children one can speak of a 'language' of art, in which certain stereotyped symbols, such as those representing the sun or a tree, stand for those objects and provide 'tokens' for them. Nadia, in contrast, did not use any tokens for objects: the symbols found in child art are entirely absent from her drawings. Again, colour is extremely important in the art of normal children, but it was totally absent from Nadia's work. And whereas most young children will draw a table with each of the four legs shown to be meeting the top, because the child is 'dominated not by what he sees but by the need to represent the relationship he knows' (Selfe 1977: 101) Nadia's drawings suggest that she was untroubled by the fact that joints between the parts of an object can be out of view.

It needs to be emphasized that Nadia's unusual drawing ability was tied to her deficiencies. The symbolic and conceptual aspects of the art of a normal child serve to make achievements such as hers impossible. In normal children, unlike Nadia, drawings represent or communicate meanings that also involve other modes of thought. The processes of cognition that underlie self-expression in art also give rise to other forms of thought and expression. Such use of identical processes to achieve different ends is essential for normal intellectual development. Its absence was a necessary (but not sufficient) condition for Nadia's skills.

Is Nadia unique? Are there no other children at all with comparable abilities? On the face of it, there is every reason to expect that at least a few other mentally handicapped children who, like Nadia, lack language skills, will share her ability to construct realistic drawings. Yet although Lorna Selfe spent a good deal of time searching for children with similar skills, she found none who matched Nadia's talents. But she did encounter a few individuals who possessed extraordinary artistic talents.

The search was extremely thorough. Lorna Selfe placed adver-
tisements in several newspapers, asking readers to help locate children
who 'have shown exceptional drawing ability at an early age'. The
several hundred replies included offers from large organizations
to examine collections and exhibitions of children's art. She also
approached all the schools for children with learning difficulties in one
large British county, all the hospitals for severely subnormal children
in the West Midlands Area Health Authority and all the schools and
units for autistic children in England.

Eventually she succeeded in locating eleven children whose drawings
demonstrated an extraordinary ability to depict objects realistically
from an early age. Some of them are discussed in a recent book in
which she specifies four particular devices that are necessary for depicting objects with literal 'photographic' realism (Selfe 1983). These are,
first, being able to show proportions within objects realistically; second,
depicting dimensions other than flat elevations; third, showing
diminishing size as distance increases; and fourth, eliminating hidden
lines. In normal children these devices are not acquired before early
adolescence, and they cannot be easily taught.

Although the search had not excluded children of normal or superior
intelligence, it emerged that all the children who were found to have
extraordinary talents for depicting objects realistically were abnormal
in other respects as well. The majority were mentally handicapped,
and almost all of them were like Nadia in having either been diagnosed
as autistic or in showing a definite tendency towards autism.

In six cases (one of whom was Nadia herself, who by then was twelve
years of age) it was possible to make a careful investigation, involving
observations of the artist and interviews with a parent or caregiver.
All six of these children showed a number of the symptoms of autism
listed in Chapter 2. Social development was retarded in all of them.
For example, in the first year of their lives they did not engage in the
usual cooing games, and they were unusually passive, crying less than
most infants. At a later stage they failed to co-operate in the games
that mothers usually play with their children, and they did not make
friendships with other children. In addition, language development
was abnormal in all six children, and one of them had no speech at all.

Furthermore, all the children had unusual mannerisms, and all were
described by their parents as having obsessions. Most of them would
sometimes persistently spin round or jump up and down on the spot,
and they all flapped their hands in a curious manner. One boy would

continuously spin objects such as pennies and screws. He also obsessively banged one note on the piano. Another child had a terror of mashed potatoes and an obsessive need for absolute tidiness. Most of them insisted on an unchanging day-to-day routine, and would have tantrums if there was the slightest change. One boy's obsessive fear of lavatories eventually led to him being hospitalized with severe constipation. A girl regularly screamed with terror whenever she heard the noise of water circulating in the radiators at her home. Busy streets or crowded places like large stores made all of them frightened or confused.

In addition to examining the drawings of these autistic children and asking parents about the manner in which their artistic abilities had developed over the years, Lorna Selfe also examined a group of normal children, mainly for purposes of comparison. The autistic children had all begun to draw a year or so later than normal chidren, and not earlier than around two-and-a-half years. Ordinary children simply scribble at first, without drawing anything recognizable. The autistic children were different: they produced recognizable objects from their very first attempts to draw. Unlike normal children, the autistic individuals hardly scribbled at all, and never doodled: their drawings were always representational (see also Mottron 1988).

The first drawings by the normal children were almost always of conventional subjects, such as people and houses. The autistic children had a wider range of subjects, but when they first started drawing they did not depict human beings. The autistic children also tended to be rigid or obsessive about their drawing instruments or the surfaces on which they drew. For example, one boy would only draw with a fine ballpoint pen, and Nadia had a similar preference (and Sacks mentions that Jose liked to draw with a fine pen, and rejected the crayons that were readily available in his ward); another would draw compulsively on any available surface, even if it was necessary to climb on the furniture in order to reach to the ceiling of his bedroom.

The autistic children spent more time in drawing than the others. They drew only to please themselves: unlike the other children they neither sought nor seemed to care about the approval of their parents. They took little notice of suggestions. The objects drawn by the autistic children were often ones in which they were highly interested or even obsessed. For example, the boy who had an obsessive fear of lavatories and had to be sent to hospital with constipation drew toilets, and another boy who had an obsession with hospitals and engaged in various kinds of self-destructive behaviour aimed at ensuring that he was hospitalized not only drew hospitals but also made models of hospital equipment. The autistic children often took their subjects from real life – they made pictures of their own homes and schools, for instance – whilst most of the normal children tended to be unadventurous and conservative in their choice of things to draw. The ordinary children preferred conventional themes and objects. These children often copied pictures or illustrations, but the autistic artists rarely did so. They drew from memory, although their drawings were often based upon or influenced by pictures they had seen. The autistic children never added decorative details to their drawings, whereas the normal children frequently included decorations and patterns.

The drawings of the autistic children document and illustrate their isolation. They are cut off from the world of other people. As I mentioned in Chapter 2, they cannot see how things must seem from another person's perspective. They appear to have no awareness of what it must be like to be another person, to be in someone else's shoes. Sacks (1985) writes that it is their 'fate' to be isolated, the exception to Donne's 'No man is an island, entire of itself', but he argues that although their inability to connect socially with others may seem to us to be a kind of death, their direct contacts with the world of physical experience provides compensation of a kind.

Is being an island, being cut off, necessarily a death? It may be a death, but it is not necessarily so. For though 'horizontal' connections with others, with society and culture, are lost, yet there may be vital and intensified 'vertical' connections, direct connections with nature, with reality, uninfluenced, unmediated, untouchable, by any others. This 'vertical' contact is very striking with Jose, hence the piercing directness, the absolute clarity of his perceptions and drawings, without a hint or shade of ambiguity or indirection, a rocklike power uninfluenced by others. (Sacks 1985: 221)

As the autistic children in Selfe's study grew older, there were some changes in their art activities. Two of the six became less interested in drawing, but two of the others, who by the time of writing were young adults, more than maintained their enthusiasm and drew something every day. When they were very young the autistic children would usually complete a drawing in a few minutes, but by adolescence those who continued to draw would devote several hours to a single picture.

Their parents reported that the normal children had all experienced difficulties in acquiring the technical devices (such as proportion and perspective) needed for depicting three-dimensional objects in two dimensions. In contrast, the autistic children learned the appropriate techniques easily, and could make use of them from a very early age. Most ordinary children will distort parts of an object they are painting or drawing in order to fit the picture on to the paper. They will sometimes 'squash' an object to get it into the space that is available. The autistic children never did this.

There are some tantalizing similarities between the drawings of autistic children such as Nadia, Jose, and the other children examined by Lorna Selfe, and some of the paleolithic and neolithic paintings that have been found in caves. Both display impressive photographic realism, and in neither is there much evidence of the considerable amounts of learning and practice that precede the ability to depict reality effectively in the figurative art of normal people. It is also interesting to note that cave art often appears in remote parts of caves, possibly indicating that the artist may have experienced little need either to communicate with others or to seek attention for his achievements. Sometimes, also, one drawing is superimposed upon another, as if the artist was insensitive (or, if not, indifferent) to whatever already appeared on the surface being used. Is it possible that autistic artists like Nadia were less rare twenty thousand years ago than they are today? We shall probably never know.

Chapter Seven

EXTRAORDINARY PEOPLE

Although mentally retarded savants may first strike us as being very peculiar individuals, on closer examination their activities display a certain logic. And their feats, albeit remarkable, are not entirely miraculous. We may have a far from complete understanding of why a mentally handicapped person chooses to follow a particular pursuit – especially when it is one which has no interest for ordinary people – or of how the person becomes capable of the achievements that so impress us, but we do know enough to perceive a degree of coherence and rationality in most of the extraordinary activities and skills that come to our attention. The circumstances that give rise to a retarded savant's achievements are not entirely different from those in which a person of normal or above average intelligence chooses to specialize in a particular area of interest. And despite the great diversity of extraordinary human abilities, the reasons for people acquiring them may be not altogether dissimilar.

On the whole, the view that mentally retarded savants are not so very different from ordinary people either in the motivation for their achievements or in the methods they bring to their tasks has proved a useful guiding assumption in our investigative efforts. Yet in some cases this assumption may be wrong and misleading. Take Nadia, for example. It is quite possible that her experience of life is fundamentally different from anything which our own experience would lead us to imagine.

But how *do* retarded savants experience their inner lives? For obvious reasons we know very little about the actual experiences of individual retarded savants. We can only observe them from the outside, seeing how they act and measuring their achievements. With the majority of retarded savants, it may be safe to assume that the

150

ways in which they experience the world are not too dissimilar from the experienced worlds of most other mentally retarded people, and not entirely different from those of ordinary people. With a minority of savants, however – a minority which would certainly include Nadia – our own experiences may be quite useless as a guide to help us imagine theirs, and it would be more fruitful to look at certain rare individuals who experience things very differently from other people.

In the previous chapter it was suggested that Nadia's world was one that was dominated by visual sensation. The direct physical qualities of objects and events were all-important: she seemed to perceive with great intensity shapes, lines, angles and dimensions where others might see only the meaning-filled objects and implications that lie beyond visual perception. But we can only make sensible guesses about this; we have no direct insight into Nadia's experiences.

Some possible hints are provided by the findings of an investigation of a man who, although very different from Nadia in most respects, shared with her the experience of having a life that was dominated by the sensory qualities of the perceived visual world, which he saw with uncanny intensity, often via images rather than direct perception. Unlike Nadia and most retarded savants, he was sufficiently intelligent and insightful to be able to describe to others his very unusual modes of experience. His reports of his life are probably much more informative than ours as a source of clues to the experienced worlds of Nadia, and perhaps to those of some other mentally retarded savants as well.

The man in question was named S.V. Shereshevskii. His abilities are described in *The Mind of a Mnemonist*, a book by the Russian psychologist, A.R. Luria (1975), who first became interested in him on account of his quite extraordinary ability to remember things. In the course of numerous interviews that extended over many years, Luria became aware that all Shereshevskii's mental life was dominated by distinct sensory impressions or images. Shereshevskii was quite incapable of having a thought that was unaccompanied by a particular physical experience of a concrete object. For instance, as he reported to Luria in 1936,

When I hear the word *green*, a green flowerpot appears; with the word *red* I see a man in a red shirt coming towards me; as for *blue*, this means an image of someone waving a small blue flag from a window. . . . Even numbers remind me of images. Take the

151

number 1. This is a proud, well-built man; 2 is a high-spirited woman; 3 a gloomy person (why I don't know); 6 a man with a swollen foot; 7 a man with a moustache; 8 a very stout woman – a sack within a sack. As for the number 87, what I see is a fat woman and a man twirling his moustache. (Luria 1975: 30)

It is important to realize that Shereshevskii did not *choose* to evoke these visual images: the domination of his thoughts by concrete physical experiences was quite involuntary. In fact, it often caused him considerable distress. Once a sensory image had been formed it was unlikely to be forgotten, ever, but although his extraordinary ability to remember was often extremely useful to him, Shereshevskii was able to make a good living as a professional mnemonist, and he amazed spectators who paid to watch performances of his powers. He was plagued by being unable to forget information that was no longer required, and by the constant presence of particular concrete images which interfered with his thinking and made it practically impossible for him to reason with abstract or general concepts.

The strong visual images he experienced also made reading very difficult for Shereshevskii. In a simple prose passage each word produced a new image, and the different images crowded in on him and often clashed with one another. Often, as the following extract illustrates, a passage would evoke a vivid image from his own childhood, distracting him from what he was trying to read.

If I'm reading a description of some palace, for some reason the main rooms always turn out to be those in an apartment I lived in as a child. . . This means I have to spend far more time with a passage if I'm to get some control of things, to reconstruct the images I see. This makes for a tremendous amount of conflict and it becomes difficult for me to read. I'm slowed down, my attention is distracted, and I can't get the important ideas in a passage. Even when I read about circumstances that are entirely new to me, if there happens to be a description, say, of a staircase, it turns out to be one in a house I once lived in. I start to follow it and lose the gist of what I'm reading. What happens is that I just can't read, can't study, for it takes up such an enormous amount of my time. (Luria 1975: 89)

Shereshevskii had his compensations, however. As well as making prodigious memory feats possible, his way of thinking in sharp visual images made it easy for him to succeed at certain kinds of problems that would be more difficult for a person who had to depend on a verbal approach. For example,

> You remember the mathematical joke: there were two books on a shelf, each 400 pages long. A bookworm gnawed through from the first page of the first volume to the last page of the second. How many pages did he gnaw through? You would no doubt say 800 – 400 pages of the first volume and 400 of the second. But I see the answer right away! He only gnaws through the two bindings. What I see is this: the two books are standing on the shelf, the first is on the left, the second to the right of it. The worm begins at the first page and keeps going to the right. But all he finds there is the binding of the first volume and that of the second. So, you see, he hasn't gnawed through anything except the two bindings. (Luria 1975: 77)

Although it is conceivable that Shereshevskii's unusual memory, and the experiences of vivid imagery which it depended upon, were influenced by his upbringing in a Jewish community which valued education and probably placed considerable emphasis on rote learning, there is little doubt that even as a young child his ways of thinking were fundamentally different from those of most people. It is probably safe to assume that the ways in which Nadia experienced the events in her environment were at least as different from the experiences of ordinary people as Shereshevskii's were, although not necessarily in the same ways. (And Shereshevskii was very different from Nadia in important respects: he was much more intelligent, for example, and better equipped to understand the meanings of things.) It is quite possible that a substantial number or retarded savants are like Shereshevskii in having thought processes or experiences which, in one way or another, are very different from those of ordinary people.

All mentally retarded savants are extraordinary in the abilities they possess. The question that now concerns us is whether a particular individual has been inherently extraordinary from the outset, having cognitive capabilities that are fundamentally abnormal, or whether the individual was at first unexceptional but *became* extraordinary as a result of learning and experience. In all probability, most people – retarded or not – who have extraordinary skills fall into the latter category. Nadia clearly seems to belong to the former category, and Shereshevskii also appears to, although we cannot be absolutely sure:

we do not not know enough about his early years. It is just possible that early experiences might somehow account for Shereshevskii's extraordinariness. In Nadia's case we can be surer in our judgement, because we know that her remarkable capacities were present at least as early as the fourth year of her life.

However extraordinary are the capacities for memory or other kinds of thinking that a person displays, it would be unwise to leap to the conclusion that the underlying mental processes must be as inherently extraordinary as Nadia's or Shereshevskii's. Their rare characteristics provide no grounds at all for thinking that extraordinary thought processes are behind all or most manifestations or extraordinary mental capacities: two swallows do not make a summer! When we are confronted with abilities that appear remarkable and bizarre, or ones that are so very extraordinary as the calendar feats and the strange number games of the twins described in Chapter 5, it is hard to avoid gaining the impression that the individuals' minds must work in very unusual ways. But a closer examination is likely to reveal that either the underlying mental processes are not, after all, entirely different from other people's, or that they became so only as a result of experience and learning.

For example, the analysis by Ian Hunter (1977) of the abilities possessed by a brilliant Edinburgh mathematician, Alexander Aitken, suggests that it is sometimes possible for extraordinary intellectual skills to emerge in a person whose inherent mental processes are essentially normal. Aitken was certainly remarkable: as well as being an eminent mathematician he possessed memory abilities that were in many respects just as impressive as Shereshevskii's. He was also an outstandingly able mental calculator and played the violin with impressive skill. According to Hunter, Aitken could

> produce a host of recondite facts about numbers, calculative methods, mathematics and mathematicians; play, on the violin, many pieces by heart; recall many musical compositions; securely identify many snatches of music heard or seen in written notation; quote extensively from English literature; and recite tracts of Latin and English verse. He could recall details of many events he had witnessed, so much so that committees often consulted him as an unofficial minute book. In daily affairs, he was conspicuously, but not obviously, precise about names, dates, locations. (Hunter 1977: 155)

154

On one occasion, when Aitken was serving in the trenches as an officer in the First World War, an important roll-book containing the names, army numbers and other details of each member of a 39–man platoon, went astray. Hunter quotes from Aitken's account of the incident.

> Batallion had rung up, requesting a list of the night's casualties and a full state of the Platoon. Apparently surnames were available, but the book was nowhere to be found. This being suddenly clear, I had no difficulty, having a well-trained memory now brought by stress into a condition almost of hypermnesia, in bringing the lost roll-book before me, almost as if it were floating; I imagined it either taken away by Mr Johnston or perhaps in the pocket of Sergeant Bree in no-man's-land. Speaking from the matting I offered to dictate the details; full name, regimental number, and the rest; they were taken down, by whom I do not know. (Aitken 1963: 107–8)

The point I wish to emphasize is that although Aitken's achievements of remembering may have been just as remarkable as Shereshevskii's, Aitken's memory, unlike Shereshevskii's, seems to have operated on basically conventional principles. Unlike Shereshevskii, and in common with many highly educated people, Aitken seems not to have depended heavily on visual imagery. He relied to a greater extent on previously gained knowledge relating to the information that he was trying to remember. And unlike Shereshevskii, Aitken did not find it particularly difficult to forget information that was no longer required, nor did he find that old memory images interfered with the acquisition of new knowledge or made comprehension difficult; and he did not have total recall of information that he had encountered years before. The weaknesses and imperfections of Aitken's memory, where they existed, were, in contrast to Shereshevskii's, similar to those of most very intelligent people. Aitken was not always able to recall, instantly, things which he could remember beforehand or subsequently. Although he was excellent at retaining certain kinds of information, his knowledge of certain subjects, such as sports, was unimpressive, and even with his areas of interest he knew less than some experts. For example, his musical knowledge was dwarfed by that of one of his acquaintances at Edinburgh University.

Like many people, Aitken was very good at remembering things that he found interesting and meaningful, and poor at remembering information that had little meaning for him. But his deep knowledge enabled him to see meanings, patterns, and structures that other people would never have noticed. As Hunter remarked,

> Aitken's memory was intimately linked with his ability to discern multiple properties that were interwoven into distinctive patterns. His discernment could work rapidly to produce an unusually rich, densely structured gestalt of properties; and so many things, that would seem chaotic to a bystander, were, to him, embodiments of multiple properties that meshed into an interesting, memorable pattern. (Hunter 1977: 157)

In order for Aitken to commit something to memory it was essential for him to concentrate totally, but also to relax. His account to Hunter provides excellent advice for others:

> Interest is the thing. Interest focuses the attention. At first one might have to concentrate, but as soon as possible one should relax. Very few people do that. Unfortunately, it is not taught at school where knowledge is acquired by rote, by learning by heart, sometimes against the grain. The thing to do is to learn by heart, not because one has to, but because one loves the thing and is interested in it. (Hunter 1977: 158)

To summarize, in some instances the extraordinary achievements of retarded savants probably depend upon the individual having a mental life which, as in the cases of Nadia and Shereshevskii, is fundamentally extraordinary in its mode of operation. In other instances extraordinary achievements do not imply the existence of underlying mental mechanisms that operate in a particularly unusual manner. The contrasting descriptions of Aitken and Shereshevskii illustrate the fact that superior individuals can be very different in this respect: the chances are that mentally retarded savants can be equally different from one another.

Retarded savants draw attention to themselves precisely because they are so different from ordinary people, but the more closely we look into what they do the more we are struck by what they have in common with everyone else. Although the strange and extraordinary aspects of savants are what first intrigue us, on further examination the commonalities begin to seem at least equally interesting. Knowing about some of the ways in which retarded savants are like other people, rather than the ways in which they are totally different, not only helps us to explain how extraordinary skills are sometimes gained by mentally retarded individuals but also provides a fund of insights into the genesis of extraordinary human talents in all kinds of people.

Making comparisons between mentally retarded savants and certain highly talented individuals can be surprisingly illuminating. For example, we might compare the early life of Harriet, the retarded Boston woman who was described in Chapter 2, with that of the composer Mozart. A comparison between the great musical genius and a mentally handicapped woman may not seem to offer much promise of being fruitful; yet there is an interesting point of contact. In Harriet's case, you may recall, music filled her surroundings from her earliest days. She spent hardly any time with other people, apart from her mother, who was far too busy giving music lessons to pay her baby daughter much attention. Music was the one constantly present element in Harriet's early life: for her it seems to have been virtually the only source of mental nourishment in an environment that was largely devoid of the interesting events and the adult attention and stimulation that most babies can count on experiencing in their homes. Music was her whole world, and she was immersed in it. For most young children, everyday events provide varied experiences of order, regularity, pattern, and movement, making it possible for the world to be perceived as one that is structured, predictable and meaningful. A child is interested in the events she perceives – especially ones that are unfamiliar – and pays them attention. As a result, much is learned about the environment, and a measure of control over it is gained. For Harriet, deprived of alternative forms of stimulation, it is possible that music on its own took on the role of conveying – but imperfectly – the experiences that most children acquire through varied sources of information. No wonder she gave music her full attention, and no wonder she learned more about music than anything else: in a sense it conveyed to her all that was significant and meaningful in her impoverished young life. Music was almost her only window on the world.

What has this to do with Mozart? However plausible the above statements about the dominant role of music in Harriet's early life may be, no one has suggested that the infant Mozart was similarly deprived. Legend has it that by some freak of chance or genetics the infant Mozart leapt into the world as a brilliant performer and a composer of genius before he reached the age of four, a miraculous *wunderkind* almost by the time he could walk. The truth is astounding enough, if not quite so miraculous. Yet, there are some interesting similarities between Mozart's early life and Harriet's. In some respects Mozart's early childhood may have been one in which he, like Harriet, was immersed in a world of music, and in which music was not simply very important for him but was made to take a dominant significance in his life, engaging his close attention for many of his waking hours.

If Harriet's total immersion in a world of musical experience came about as an accidental outcome of her being deprived of other kinds of experience, Mozart's was a result of a deliberate policy on the part of his father, Leopold Mozart. Leopold, who was a musician of some ability, and an experienced music teacher, was exceedingly ambitious on behalf of his son, and we went to immense lengths to help develop the child's abilities and draw the world's attention to them. Frustrated in his own ambitions, and self-righteously claiming that he sacrificed himself for his son, Leopold 'dedicated his life to making his son into an important musician in the best way he knew' (Hildesheimer 1983: 67), even if it meant the son receiving endless obligatory lessons, and having to practise and practise until he could not keep his eyes open. The determined and single-minded Leopold had already had a great deal of success teaching his son's older sister, Nannerl. If the young Mozart had not been successful, it would not have been through lack of effort on the part of his father! The child did not play outdoors like other children, and was given little chance to get to know other children. One suspects that from his very earliest years the majority of the time was spent on musical activities that were carefully planned by the father. From the age of only six the young Mozart, with his sister, was dragged all over Europe by Leopold, who seems to have had few qualms about exploiting his children's talents.

The impression given by Leopold that his son's performances were effortless, and the accuracy of Leopold's transpositions of music that he claimed his four-year-old-son had composed entirely on his own, need to be assessed in the light of the knowledge that the father was not above the occasional minor duplicity if it might make his son's achievements appear to be even more astounding than they actually were, and consequently lead to an increase in the profits received from the child's performances. For three and a half years the two children were constantly on the move, playing everywhere:

> Like a coin-operated mechanical clock, the two performed for anyone who handed the entrance fee to Leopold, the cashier. As

a special feature they played on covered keys or sight-read whatever music a listener might have brought along. For this there was no extra charge. In order to increase the sensational aspect of their act, Leopold reduced the children's ages by one year on the announcements. Indeed, these read like circus posters. (Hildesheimer 1983: 31)

The young Mozart was a compliant child. He loved his father, was willing to be controlled by him and anxious to please him, and he tolerated and possibly even enjoyed the unnaturally arduous regime his father arranged for him. Undoubtedly the life of a child prodigy had its rewards, even if he was expected to act more like a little adult machine than a human child.

Pointing out that Harriet shared with Mozart the early experience of total immersion in a life of music does not explain Mozart's genius, of course. But the existence of a state of affairs in which one is immersed in an interest that is engulfing, constantly in mind, and intently pursued for much of one's time, day after day, month after month and year after year, is something that is regularly encountered in connection with prodigious feats of learning by individuals at every level of ability. When Gauss was asked how he obtained his mastery over numbers, he replied, 'By always thinking about them.' Retarded savants are in many respects unlike Gauss or any other great mathematician, of course, and equally unlike the Mozarts and Bachs and Beethovens of this world, or the Darwins and Einsteins, but they do share with them – and this, more than any other single factor, provides the key to the savant achievements we marvel at – the capacity to be constantly and wholeheartedly engrossed in whatever they put their minds to, to concentrate and drive out distractions and competing interests, in short, to inhabit for long periods of time a mental world in which nothing but the object of their interest, or perhaps obsession, is allowed to exist.

Such a capacity for a person to be fully committed to one particular interest, and totally engulfed in it to the extent that most of one's energies are directed towards it throughout the waking hours, is likely to be encountered in any kind of person (irrespective of that individual's level of general competence) who displays abilities that are genuinely remarkable. In intelligent people it is usually accompanied by considerably more self-awareness and conscious decision-making than a mentally retarded person would be capable of: intelligent scholars, scientists and artists are better equipped than mentally handicapped individuals to decide what they are going to specialize in, and their day-to-day activities are more likely to be guided by a sense of direction and to have long-term goals or plans that they wish to fulfil.

In a scholar like Aitken we can see, in combination, both the immersion in particular interests that retarded savants and outstandingly talented individuals have in common, and also the planning ability and sense of direction that only the latter possess. These two essential elements of high-level achievements – being completely immersed in an interest and having long-term plans – are usually encountered together, in tandem, but at different stages in a person's life the relative importance of each may alter. We see this, for example, in the early and later lives of George Parker Bidder, a notable mid-nineteenth century engineer, who as an adult was a friend of Brunel and Robert Stephenson and made important contributions to a large number of engineering projects. Robert Stephenson spoke with warmth and admiration of his mental capacities and his 'pure analytical mind'. Bidder's success as a mature man clearly depended on both the qualities we have emphasized – first, becoming immersed in one's subject and, second, being able to plan and direct one's achievements. But he was also very exceptional as a young child, and at that stage the first of the two qualities was the crucial one, and the second one, if not inessential, was not nearly as important as it was to be later.

Bidder's early success was as a child prodigy who had an extraordinary ability to perform rapid calculations by mental arithmetic. He was known as 'The Calculating Boy'. Some of his later statements help us to understand how and why he became so successful at mental calculations, despite his own insistence that he had no particular aptitude for mathematics. According to his biographer, E.G. Clark, a lecture given by Bidder in his forties provides,

> A picture of a small boy lying in bed at night listening to his family discussing and making calculations about the purchases and bargains which, in their humble circumstances, were of great importance to them; of his brother teaching him to count up to a hundred, of the boy himself counting and making discoveries about numbers: that it is quicker to count to 100 by counting, to ten, ten times over, than to repeat the long names, twenty-one, twenty-two, and so on . . . . He learns to add: 6 and 6 is the same as 6 and 4 and 2, which is the same as 10 and 2, which is 12. 'This was the

means', he says, 'that my uninstructed mind took'. He practises, and thinks about numbers continually, hardly realizing that in doing this he is at all exceptional (Clark 1983: 316–17).

At an early stage it was made clear to Bidder that his interest in numbers could be useful, and perhaps even profitable, and he began to receive a good deal of encouragement from his parents and other adults. His family first realized that he could do mental calculations on an occasion when, lying in bed, he overheard a dispute about the price and weight of a pig and called down to tell them what the correct price should be. Soon afterwards, on an evening when he was with an elderly blacksmith who allowed him to play in his workshop, and occasionally blow the bellows, and listen to the blacksmith's stories:

> On one of these occasions, somebody by chance mentioned a sum; . . . I gave the answer correctly. This occasioned some little astonishment; they then asked me other questions, which I answered with equal facility. They then went on to ask me up to two place of figure . . . of course I did not do it then as rapidly as afterwards, but I gave the answer correctly, as was verified by the old gentleman's nephew, who began chalking it up to see if I was right. As a natural consequence this increased my fame still more, and what was better, it eventually caused halfpence to flow into my pocket; which, I need not say, had the effect of attaching me still more to the science of arithmetic, and thus by degrees I got on . . . . (G.H. Bidder, quoted by Clark 1983: 5).

Lacking formal education, Bidder was not taught the conventional written methods of arithmetic calculations such as long multiplication and division. So far as mental calculating was concerned this was an advantage since, as Bidder pointed out, the easiest method for, say, mental multiplication is very different from the one that is used for multiplying on paper. He explained in a lecture that in order to do complicated multiplications by mental arithmetic it is necessary to use a procedure in which only one result has to be held in memory at a time. One way of making this possible is to begin with the left-hand digit in the multiplier and add the partial products in succession. For example, to multiply 279 x 373 Bidder would start by multiplying 200 x 300, and to the product of that (60,000) add, successively, the products of 200 x 70, 200 x 3, 70 x 300, 70 x 70, 70 x 3, 9 x 300, 9 x 70, and 9 x 3, to give the total, 104,067.

Bidder explained how necessary it was for him to have procedures for calculating in which only one intermediate answer needed to be held in memory at a time, and he insisted that he did not have an unusually good ability to remember. It was also important to him to have a great amount of knowledge about particular numbers, their various properties, attributes and qualities. Like Aitken, Bidder felt that there was nothing intrinsically extraordinary about the working of his mind: both Bidder and Aitken attributed their success to the use of effective methods, extensive knowledge of numbers, and immersion in their interest and sustained concentration.

Bidder developed his numerical skills in a number of directions. An especially impressive achievement was his discovery at the age of about twelve of a method to calculate compound interest by mental arithmetic. In childhood he gave exhibitions of his talents which attracted considerable attention to him as a child prodigy, earned needed money and, most importantly, led to offers of help with his education, making it possible for him to gain the achievements of his highly successful adult life.

Both Bidder and Aitken were hugely talented individuals. Yet in each case, although at first sight it might appear that there must have existed mental abilities that were as fundamentally different from those of ordinary people as Shereshevskii's and Nadia's seem to have been, closer examination makes it appear more likely that their intellectual powers were not fundamentally extraordinary, and that their achievements, which were extraordinary, were the outcome of an essentially normal mental-processing capacity allied to unusually intense and long-lasting attention, concentration and involvement in particular interests, and, partly in consequence, an exceptional amount of knowledge about and familiarity with all concepts and items of information that were at all relevant to their areas of special interest.

The fact that neither Bidder nor Aitken appear to have been so extraordinary in their basic mental capacities as Nadia and Shereshevskii does not rule out the possibility that certain other talented individuals have shared the latter's mental peculiarities, whether or not that is also true of some mentally retarded savants. The achievements of neither Bidder nor Aitken were quite as dependent upon memory, as such, as Shereshevskii's were. Is it possible that those outstandingly talented individuals who do depend upon extraordinary memorizing achievements need to be, at least in respect to memory processes, more like Shereshevskii than either Bidder or Aitken seem to have been? The famous English historian, politician and legislator, Thomas Babbington Macaulay, who was phenomenally successful at remembering numerous lengthy passages of verse and prose, provides a suitable instance of a person for whom this suggestion might be applicable.

Of all the outstandingly able scholars who have lived, Macaulay, whose feats of memory were legendary, would seem to have been as likely as anyone to have possessed a capacity for remembering that was fundamentally extraordinary. He knew by heart large numbers of poems, including exceedingly long ones such as *Paradise Lost* which has 10,565 lines, and he could also remember substantial parts of a number of Shakespeare's plays and numerous lengthy prose passages as well.

But extraordinary as Macaulay's memory feats undoubtedly were, knowing something of his style of life, of his background, his interests and his values makes it clear that the feats were not quite so bizarre or inexplicable as they might otherwise appear. Throughout his life, the written word was all-important for Macaulay, and it was also very necessary for him to be able to learn long passages by heart. He came from a literary background 'where books were continually read and discussed, where exact and apposite quotation was an everyday part of conversation and letter writing, where the learning of passages by heart was both commonplace and valued' (Hunter 1985: 227). Among his friends, and the people he associated with, the memorization of long text passages was admired and praised: the social climate Macaulay inhabited was one in which he was strongly encouraged for working very hard at memory tasks. And books surrounded him: his world was a world of books. When he was not sleeping he was usually reading or writing a book.

In short, books for Macaulay were the main interest in his life, and many of his activities contributed in one way or another to his mastery of literary knowledge. This is the light in which his memory achievements should be viewed: they were not arbitrary feats or something to be added on to his other accomplishments. Rather, they were a central element in a life which was committed to books and written knowledge. Against this background memorizing must have seemed a perfectly natural activity, and one to which Macaulay would have thought it reasonable to devote a very substantial proportion of his time. It was also an activity at which being successful had a good deal of practical utility, was likely to elicit the admiration of others, and was necessary for his own self-esteem. So there were many excellent reasons for Macaulay's excellence at remembering: his achievements can be understood without invoking any fundamentally unusual mental processes. Although it cannot be proved or disproved, the chances are that in contrast to Shereshevskii's memory, Macaulay's operated on roughly the same lines as the memories of most people whose ability to recall information is not at all extraordinary.

There are certain other rare human accomplishments which, it might appear, would only be possible if the individual concerned had very special intellectual powers. For instance, consider the case of Sir Richard Burton, the nineteenth-century British linguist, anthropologist, poet, explorer and soldier. Of this famous Victorian's many achievements, perhaps the best known are his explorations in search of the origins of the Nile, his visit to Mecca, and his translations into English of *The Arabian Nights* and many other works of eastern literature. Almost all of Burton's accomplishments depended to some extent on the fact that he was a quite outstandingly able linguist: he is reported to have mastered around forty different languages, and a number of dialects as well.

Burton's ability to learn foreign languages was so exceptional that there would seem to be no way of accounting for it unless he possessed some special innate talent for language acquisition. Learning three or four different languages is a considerable achievement: a total of forty seems well beyond the capacity of any ordinary mortal! So we are strongly tempted to decide that the sheer exceptionality of Burton's achievements, ones that would appear to be outside what is humanly possible, provide a very strong case for claiming that Burton's mental capacities must have been extraordinary from the outset.

But as in Macaulay's case, a closer examination of the man, his interests, ambitions, values and his style of life, suggests that this conclusion may not be justified after all. A knowledge of Burton's life provides us with two strong reasons for questioning it. First, his own journals make it very clear that he did not find language learning at all easy, that the methods and techniques he followed were not unusual, and that the only quality that really did set him apart from other learners was his prodigious capacity for hard work: he was extremely determined and had enormous powers of persistence, his doggedness and sheer energy, and his willingness to submit himself constantly to long and arduous hours of work at learning tasks, were indisputably extraordinary. But that kind of extraordinariness is clearly very different from having radically special mental capabilities.

Second, Burton was extraordinary in the extent to which, throughout his life, he received encouragement and rewards for his persistence at learning new languages. In his childhood, his family spent several years wandering between different parts of Europe. He was a gregarious boy, and was often in the position of badly wanting to communicate with people who spoke different languages from his. So from an early age he put a good deal of effort into learning foreign languages, and that effort was speedily rewarded. His early successes gave him the encouragement he needed to persevere with new challenges. As he grew into adolescence and adulthood, his way of life and his interests, and his need to make a living for himself, repeatedly placed him in situations where it would be valuable for him to learn yet another language. In such circumstances, where another person might have lacked the determination or the confidence to take on what was obviously going to be a very difficult and time-consuming burden of learning, and one with a doubtful likelihood of eventual success, Burton saw things differently. He had done it before, and the results had justified the effort. He knew that he could do it again.

So with Burton, like Macaulay, we are in the position of seeing that however extraordinary the accomplishments that come to our attention, it is quite possible that they can be accounted for by the fact that the circumstances of life were unusually favourable ones for certain kinds of learning achievements. In neither case need the possibility of fundamentally extraordinary mental capacities be ruled out, but in each of them the most parsimonious stance is to assume that, in the absence of an established necessity for such special powers, they probably did not exist. This is not true in Shereshevskii's case, or Nadia's, so far as we can tell. Is it true of Mozart? That is not an easy question to answer.

If I was asked to make a brief general statement about the prerequisites of extraordinary learned abilities – a statement that would be intended to apply to highly intelligent and mentally retarded individuals alike – it would be this:

People are likely to gain an unusual degree of competence at an area of mental expertise if they become sufficiently interested in it to devote a substantial proportion of their time towards it, giving it their undivided attention and eventually building up a body of relevant knowledge and necessary mental skills.

Can the causes of human excellence be quite that simple, and so very humdrum as that bald statement suggests? Is it really true that human excellence can be reduced to motivation, attention, time and effort, as the statement implies? Hasn't something crucial been left out? For instance, what about the contributions of innate talents and inherited abilities?

I suspect that the statement above comes closer to being true than most psychologists would think. But it undoubtedly oversimplifies the true state of affairs: at best it is a caricature which omits all the complexities and subtleties. And it raises as many questions as it answers. For instance, it does not begin to explain how a person can *become* 'sufficiently interested' in something to devote to it all the time and attention that is needed. It does not say how an individual can gain that all-important commitment, self-confidence, sense of purpose and direction. All the same, if the statement is a fundamentally correct one, albeit a simplified account of the causes of exceptional feats of learning and memory, it at least helps to specify the directions we should move in if we wish to encourage people to acquire high levels of expertise. If it is really true, as the statement implies, that what people *achieve* largely depends on what they *do*, the implications are clear enough.

But many would argue that the brief statement above is not just oversimplified but quite wrong. They would claim that abilities and achievements depend not only on what people do, but, at least as importantly, on what they are, on their having, or not having, natural, inherited, innate talents. If this latter view is correct, all the attention, effort, motivation, commitment, involvement and sense of direction in the world will not be enough for a person to succeed at a mental task, unless nature has imbued that individual with suitable genes and the appropriate innate talents. As it happens, although there are strong reasons for asserting that unlearned individual differences affect people's chances of success at various learned skills, the issues involved in trying to verify such an assertion are extremely complex: I shall confine my remarks to some brief comments.

Essentially, there are two related claims. The first is that outstanding mental achievements are only possible if certain innate talents are present. The second claim is that such achievements always depend on inherited characteristics which differ from one person to another: the right genes must be present.

The argument that certain mental achievements are only possible when necessary innate talents exist is widely accepted, plausible, and may well be entirely correct. But 'innate talents' are not defined independently of the achievements that are cited as evidence for the existence of such talents. This leads to circular reasoning, as in the following exchange:

Question	Why is X good at music?
Answer	Because she has a talent for it.
Question	How do you know she has a talent for music?
Answer	Because she is good at it.

We are left asking, 'What exactly *is* a talent?' The circularity demonstrated in the dialogue above can be avoided if a talent is defined as some kind of prerequisite skill, or 'potentiality' or 'tendency' that is necessary in order for an achievement to be possible, so long as it is possible to define and measure the skill, potentiality or tendency independently of the achievement that it is said to cause. Unfortunately, this has never been done, although we come fairly near to defining talents satisfactorily with occasional statements about necessary precursors of exceptionality. For example, it is sometimes claimed that perfect auditory pitch perception may be a necessary prerequisite for certain musical achievements, and can be observed very early in a child's life. Since it is possible to measure a child's pitch perception independently of later musical achievement, it would seem to qualify as a possible talent that can be properly defined and measured, avoiding the circularity encountered above.

As it happens, the view that having had perfect pitch perception in early childhood is a necessary attribute of outstanding musicians may be wrong. In a study of twenty-one outstandingly successful young performers who were beginning careers as concert pianists it was found that whilst sensitivity to sound and good pitch discrimination were regarded as valuable assets, only some of the pianists had these qualities to a high degree at an early age (Bloom 1985). Moreover, among young adults who had reached the highest levels of achievement in a number of different areas of endeavour, it turned out that only rarely had the individuals in the study been given their initial instruction in the talent field because the parents or teachers saw unusual gifts in the young child (Bloom 1985: 544). Of course, none of this evidence proves that innate talents are either unimportant or non-existent, but it does indicate that the truth of the assertion that innate talents are a necessary cause of certain human achievements cannot be taken for granted.

And it is essential that any explanation that invokes innate talents as causes is accompanied by an explicit statement about the precise form of such talents.

The argument for inherited influences rests on firmer ground. There is strong evidence that abilities are affected by genetic factors. However, we have very little understanding of the mechanisms by which genetic factors actually affect the acquisition of human abilities. It is important to know about this, because until we do we are in no position to decide what practical steps, if any, may be taken in order to remedy defects that are caused by genetic circumstances being less than ideal. To illustrate this point, imagine a situation in which it is known only that due to some unspecified genetic cause, some people are better at needlework than others. In the absence of any further knowledge we would be unable to say how best to improve the needleworking skills of those people who are not, genetically, well endowed. But if we were to discover that mechanism (via which genetic factors lead to individual differences in needlework) was, say, the visual perception system, we would be placed in a much better position to help, for example by providing spectacles for those people who (for genetic reasons) needed them most.

To conclude, in this book I have tried to explain how the combined findings of numerous psychological investigations of retarded people make it possible for us to have a reasonably full understanding of how and why a few mentally retarded people have been able to gain some remarkable skills and abilities. Of course, many questions that cannot be readily answered have been raised, not only concerning the particular skills of retarded savants but also about wider issues in the psychology of cognition. Among all the findings, the point that emerges most forcibly, most repeatedly and perhaps most importantly is that many human abilities can operate with a greater degree of autonomy and independence than they are supposed to possess. The prevailing view that particular intellectual skills are constrained by an all-pervading general level of ability or intelligence has turned out to be something of a myth.

Bibliography

Aitken, A.C. (1963) *Gallipoli to the Somme: recollections of a New Zealand infantryman*, London: Oxford University Press.

Anastasi, A. and Levee, R.F. (1960) 'Intellectual defect and musical talent: a case report', *American Journal of Mental Deficiency* 64: 659–705.

Aram, D.M. and Healy, J.M. (1988) 'Hyperlexia: a review of extraordinary word recognition', in L.K. Obler and D. Fein (eds) *The Exceptional Brain: Neuropsychology of Talent and Special Abilities*, New York: The Guilford Press.

Baron-Cohen, S., Leslie, A.M., and Frith, U. (1985) 'Does the autistic child have a "theory of mind"?', *Cognition* 21: 37–46.

Belmont, J.M. (1978) 'Individual differences in memory: the cases of normal and retarded development', in M.M. Gruneberg and P.E. Morris (eds) *Aspects of Memory*, London: Methuen.

Bennett, H.L. (1983) 'Remembering drink orders: the memory skills of cocktail waitresses', *Human Learning: Journal of Practical Research and Application* 2: 157–70.

Bettelheim, B. (1959) 'Joey: a "mechanical boy"', *Scientific American* 200: March, 116–30.

Bloom, B.S. (ed.) (1985) *Developing Talent in Young People*, New York: Ballantine Books.

Boygo, L. and Ellis, R. (1988) 'Elly: a study in contrasts', in L. K. Obler and D. Fein (eds) *The Exceptional Brain: Neuropsychology of Talent and Special Abilities*, New York: The Guilford Press.

Brill, A.A. (1940) 'Some peculiar manifestations of memory with special reference to lightning calculators', *Journal of Nervous and Mental Diseases* 92: 709–26.

Bronfenbrenner, U. (1979) *The Ecology of Human Development*, Cambridge, Massachusetts: Harvard University Press.

Byrd, H. (1920) 'A case of phenomenal memorizing by a feeble-minded negro', *Journal of Applied Psychology* 4: 202–6.

Cain, A.C. (1969) 'Special "isolated" abilities in severely psychotic young children', *Psychiatry* 32: 137–47.

Ceci, S.J. and Howe, M.J.A. (1978) 'Semantic knowledge as a

determinant of developmental differences in recall', *Journal of Experimental Child Psychology* 26: 230–45.

Charness, N., Clifton, J. and Macdonald, L. (1988) 'Case study of a musical "mono-savant": a cognitive-psychological focus', in L. K. Obler and D. Fein (eds) *The Exceptional Brain: Neuropsychology of Talent and Special Abilities*, New York: The Guilford Press.

Chase, W.G. and Ericsson, K.A. (1981) 'Skilled memory', in J.R. Anderson (ed.) *Cognitive Skills and their Acquisition*, Hillsdale, New Jersey: Erlbaum.

Chi, M.T.H. (1978) 'Knowledge structures and memory development', in R. Siegler (ed.) *Children's Thinking: What Develops?* Hillsdale, New Jersey: Erlbaum.

Clark, E.F. (1983) *George Parker Bidder: The Calculating Boy*, Bedford: KSL Publications.

Craik, F.I.M. and Tulving, E. (1975) 'Depth of processing and the retention of words in episodic memory', *Journal of Experimental Psychology: General* 104: 268–94.

Darwin, C. (1958), *The Autobiography of Charles Darwin, 1809–1882* (with original omissions restored) edited by N. Barlow, London: Collins.

Dennett, D. (1983) 'Artificial intelligence and the strategies of psychological investigation', in J. Miller (ed.) *States of Mind*, London: BBC.

Deutsch, D. (1975) 'The organization of short-term memory for a single acoustic attribute', in D. Deutsch and J.A. Deutsch (eds) *Short-term Memory*, New York: Academic Press.

Estes, W.K. (1970) *Learning Theory and Mental Development*, New York: Academic Press.

Feldman, D.H. (1982) 'A developmental framework for research with gifted children', in D.H. Feldman (ed.) *Developmental Approaches to Giftedness and Creativity*, New Directions for Child Development, No. 17, September, San Francisco: Josey-Bass.

Fodor, J.A. (1983) *The Modularity of Mind*, Cambridge, Massachusetts: MIT Press.

Forrest, D.V. (1969) 'New words and neologisms: with a thesaurus of coinages by a schizophrenic savant', *Psychiatry* 32: 44–73.

Forrest, D.W. (1974) *Francis Galton: the life and work of a Victorian genius*, London: Elek.

Gardner, H. (1975) *The Man with a Shattered Mind*, New York: Knopf.

Gardner, H. (1984) *Frames of Mind*, London: Heinemann.

Gazzaniga, M.S. and LeDoux, J.E. (1978) *The Integrated Mind*, New York: Plenum.

Geschwind, N. (1983) 'The organisation of the living brain', in J. Miller (ed.) *States of Mind: conversations with psychological investigators*, London: BBC.

Gladwin, T. (1970) *East is a Big Bird: navigation and logic on Puluwat Atoll*, Cambridge, Massachusetts: Harvard University Press.

Goldsmith, L.T. and Feldman, D.H. (1988) 'Idiots savants – thinking about remembering: a response to White', *New Ideas in Psychology* 6: 15–23.

Goodenough, F. (1926) *Measurement of Intelligence by Drawings*, New York: Harcourt, Brace and World.

Goodman, J. (1972) 'A case study of an "autistic-savant": mental function in the psychotic child with markedly discrepant abilities', *Journal of Child Psychology and Psychiatry* 13: 267–78.

Haber, R.N. (1979) 'Twenty years of haunting eidetic imagery: where's the ghost?', *Behavioral and Brain Sciences* 2: 583–629.

Hermelin, B. (1976) 'Coding and the sense modalities', in L. Wing (ed.) *Early Childhood Autism*, New York: Pergamon.

Hermelin, B. and O'Connor, N. (1970) *Psychological Experiments with Autistic Children*, Oxford: Pergamon.

Hildesheimer, W. (1983) *Mozart* (translated from the German by Marion Faber), London: Dent.

Hill, A.L. (1974) 'Idiots savants: a categorization of abilities', *Mental Retardation* 12: 12–13.

Hill, A.L. (1975) 'An investigation of calendar calculating by an idiot savant', *American Journal of Psychiatry* 132: 557–60.

Hill, A.L. (1977) 'Idiots savants: rate of incidence', *Perceptual and Motor Skills* 44: 161–2.

Hill, A.L. (1978) 'Savants: mentally retarded individuals with special skills', in N.R. Ellis (ed.) *International Review of Research in Mental Retardation*, vol. 9, New York: Academic Press.

Horwitz, W.A., Deming, W.E., and Winter, R.F. (1969) 'A further account of the idiots savants, experts with the calendar', *American Journal of Psychiatry* 126: 160–3.

Horwitz, W.A., Kestenbaum, C., Person, E., and Jarvik, L. (1965) 'Identical twin – "idiot savants" – calendar calculators', *American Journal of Psychiatry* 121: 1075–9.

Howe, M.J.A. (1989) 'Cognitive processes in "idiots savants"', in A.M. Colman and G. Beaumont (eds) *Psychology Survey 7*, Leicester: The British Psychological Society.

Howe, M.J.A. and Smith, J. (1988) 'Calendar calculating in "idiots savants": how do they do it?', *British Journal of Psychology* 79: 371–86.

Hunter, I.M.L. (1977) 'An exceptional memory', *British Journal of Psychology* 68: 155–64.

Hunter, I.M.L. (1985) 'Lengthy verbatim recall: the role of text', in A. Ellis (ed.) Progress in the Psychology of Language, vol. 1, Hillsdale, New Jersey: Erlbaum.

Huttenlocher, P.R. and Huttenlocher, J. (1973) 'A study of children with hyperlexia', *Neurology* 23: 1107–16.

Jaynes, J. (1976) *The Origins of Consciousness in the Breakdown of the Bicameral Mind*, New York: Houghton Mifflin.

Jones, H.E. (1926) 'Phenomenal memorizing as a "special ability"', *Journal of Applied Psychology* 10: 367–77.

Kahr, B.E. and Neisser, U. (1982) The Cognitive Strategies of a

Calendar Calculator, unpublished manuscript, Cornell University.

LaFontaine, L. (1974) Divergent Abilities in the Idiot Savant, Ed. D. thesis, Boston University (Ann Arbor: University Microfilms Inc., 1982).

Leslie, A.M. and Frith, U. (1988) 'Autistic children's understanding of seeing, knowing and believing', *British Journal of Developmental Psychology* 6: 315–24.

Lindsley, O.R. (1965) 'Can deficiency produce specific superiority? The challenge of the idiot savant', *Exceptional Children* 31: 225–32.

Lucci, D., Fein, D., Holevas, A. and Kaplan, E. (1988) 'Paul: a musically gifted autistic boy', in L.K. Obler and D. Fein (eds) *The Exceptional Brain: Neuropsychology of Talent and Special Abilities*, New York: The Guilford Press.

Luria, A.R. (1975) *The Mind of a Mnemonist*, translated from the Russian by Lynn Solotaroff, Harmondsworth: Penguin.

McClelland, D.C. (1973) 'Testing for competence rather than for "intelligence"', *American Psychologist* 28: 1–14.

Mehegan, C.C. and Dreifuss, F.E. (1972) 'Hyperlexia: exceptional reading ability in brain-damaged children', *Neurology* 22: 1105–11.

Mehler, J., Morton, J., and Jusczyk, P.W. (1984) 'On reducing language to biology', *Cognitive Neuropsychology* 1: 83–116.

Miller, L.K. (1987) 'Determinants of melody span in a developmentally disabled musical savant', *Psychology of Music* 15: 76–89.

Morishima, A. (1974) '"Another Van Gogh of Japan": the superior artwork of a retarded boy', *Exceptional Children* 41: 92–6.

Morishima, A. and Brown, L.F. (1976) 'An idiot savant case report: a retrospective view', *Mental Retardation* 14: 46–7.

Morris, P.E., Gruneberg, M.M., Sykes, R.N. and Merrick, A. (1981) 'Football knowledge and the acquisition of new results', *British Journal of Psychology* 72: 479–83.

Mottron, L. (1988) Developmental peculiarities of graphic recall in an Asperger's Syndrome subject with good visual memory. Paper presented at Nato Advanced Study Institute, Savoy, on Social Competence in Developmental Perspective.

Nurcombe, B. and Parker, N. (1964) 'The idiot savant', *Journal of American Academy of Child Psychiatry* 3: 469–87.

O'Connor, N. and Hermelin, B. (1989) 'The memory structure of autistic idiot-savant mnemonists', *British Journal of Psychology* 80: 97–111.

Owens, W.A. and Grimm, W. (1941) 'A note regarding exceptional musical ability in a low-grade imbecile', *Journal of Educational Psychology* 33: 636–7.

Palo, J. and Kivalo, A. (1977) 'Calendar calculator with progressive mental deficiency', *Acta Paedopsychiatrica* 42: 227–31.

Parker, S.W. (1917) 'A pseudo-talent for words: the teacher's report to Dr Witmer', *The Psychological Clinic* 11: 1–17.

Premack, D. and Woodruff, G. (1978) 'Does the chimpanzee have a "theory of mind"?', *Behavioral and Brain Sciences* 4: 515–26.

Prior, M.R. (1979) 'Cognitive abilities and disabilities in infantile autism: a review', *Journal of Abnormal Child Psychology* 7: 357–80.

Rife, D.C. and Snyder, L.H. (1931) *Human Biology* 3: 547–59.

Rimland, B. (1964) *Infantile Autism: the syndrome and its implications for a neural theory of behavior*, New York: Appleton-Centruy Crofts.

Rimland, B. (1978) 'Savant capabilities of autistic children and their cognitive implications', in G. Serban (ed.) *Cognitive Deficits in the Development of Mental Illness*, New York: Brunner/Mazel.

Roberts, A.D. (1945) 'Case history of a so-called idiot savant', *Journal of Genetic Psychology* 66: 259–65.

Robinson, J.F. and Vitale, L.J. (1954) 'Children with circumscribed interest patterns', *American Journal of Orthopsychiatry* 24: 755–66.

Rozin, P. (1976) 'The evolution of intelligence and access to the cognitive unconscious', *Progress in Psychobiology and Physiological Psychology* 6: 245–80.

Rutter, M. (1978) 'Diagnosis and definition', in M. Rutter and E. Schopler (eds) *Autism: a reappraisal of concepts of treatment*, New York: Plenum.

Sacks, O. (1985) *The Man who Mistook his Wife for a Hat*, London: Duckworth.

Scheerer, M., Rothmann, E. and Goldstein, K. (1945) 'A case of "idiot savant": an experimental study of personality organization', *Psychological Monographs* 58 (4), no. 269: 1–63.

Selfe, L. (1977) *Nadia: a case of extraordinary drawing ability in an autistic child*, London: Academic Press.

Selfe, L. (1983) *Normal and Anomalous Representational Drawing Ability in Children*, London: Academic Press.

Sloboda, J.A., Hermelin, B. and O'Connor, N. (1985) 'An exceptional musical memory', *Music Perception* 3: 155–70.

Smith, J. and Howe, M.J.A. (1985) 'An investigation of calendar-calculating skills in an "idiot savant"', *International Journal of Rehabilitation Research* 8: 77–9.

Stern, M.-E. and Maire, M. (1937) 'Un cas d'aptitude speciale de dessin chèz un imbécile', *Archives de Medecine des Enfants* 40: 458–60.

Sternberg, R.J. and Salter, W. (1982) 'Conceptions of intelligence', in R.J. Sternberg (ed.) *Handbook of Human Intelligence*, Cambridge: Cambridge University Press.

Stevenson, H.W., Parker, T. and Wilkinson, A. (1975) Ratings and Measures of Memory Processes in Young Children, unpublished manuscript, University of Michigan.

Treffert, D.A. (1989) *Extraordinary People*, New York: Harper & Row.

Viscott, D.S. (1970) 'A musical idiot savant', *Psychiatry* 33: 494–515.

Waterhouse, L. (1988) 'Extraordinary visual memory and pattern perception in an autistic boy', in L.K. Obler and D. Fein (eds) *The Exceptional Brain: Neuropsychology of Talent and Special Abilities*, New York: The Guilford Press.

Weiskrantz, L., Warrington, E.K., Sanders, D.M. and Marshall, J.

(1974) 'Visual capacity in the hemianopic field following restricted occipital ablation', *Brain* 97: 709–15.

White, P.A. (1988) 'The structured representation of information in long-term memory: a possible explanation for the accomplishments of "idiots savants"', *New Ideas in Psychology* 6: 3–14.

Wiener, N. (1953) *Ex-Prodigy: my childhood and youth*, New York: Simon & Schuster.

Zigler, E. and Seitz, V. (1982) 'Social policy and intelligence', in R.J. Sternberg (ed.) *Handbook of Human Intelligence*, Cambridge: Cambridge University Press.

AUTHOR INDEX

SUBJECT INDEX